Women Short-Changed

by History

by
Barbara Venton Montgomery, Ph. D.

Heritage Books, Inc.
Bowie, Maryland
1998

Copyright 1998
Barbara Venton Montgomery

Cover Illustration by Lee Ashlin

Published 1998 by

HERITAGE BOOKS, INC.
1540E Pointer Ridge Place
Bowie, Maryland 20716
1-800-398-7709
http://www.heritagebooks.com

ISBN: 0-7884-0991-3

A Complete Catalog Listing Hundreds of Titles
On History, Genealogy, and Americana
Available Free Upon Request

INTRODUCTION

Although there are many unread books on the shelves of college and university libraries on the suffrage movement or on early feminists, few contain the names of all five of my ladies in **Women Short-Changed by History**. Nor do these books address the personality and motivation of the women involved. They are merely short biographical sketches with a few brief facts and dates.

All of my ladies were strong and independent when women were supposed to be dependent and weak. They knew how they wanted to live their lives, and they did so. Sometimes their choices were not the best, and certainly they were not what was anticipated of women for their period in history. But, all five of my ladies accepted the responsibility for their actions and went ahead with their lives. If they regretted anything they did, not one of them said, "Sorry about that," although The Woodhull simply denied she did or said the things she did and said.

Pocahontas was stoic and accepting of her imminent death. Lucy Terry Prince was active and enjoying life until the end. Mary Edwards Walker was trying (unsuccessfully) to fulfill her dreams until her last breath. Victoria Woodhull kept ordering people while defying death by sitting upright in her chair, refusing to even consider dying in bed. And, Sarah Josepha Hale edited *Godey's* until she was 89.

As I encountered bits and pieces of their lives while teaching history for more than fifty years, I became somewhat obsessed with them and needed to know more about these five women.

I began collecting books, monographs, and newspaper articles to gain insights into their actions. I got to know them well. I believe I would have wanted them for friends, except, perhaps for Victoria Woodhull with her large unruly family, lovers, and husbands. Even with all these people surrounding her, Victoria was still a "loner." Only Sarah Josepha Hale enjoyed society. Perhaps she would be considered the only lady among the five.

They decided their future. None of them have been given sufficient credit for what they achieved in pursuit of their dreams. Hopefully, this book will remedy that.

Author's Note:

The bibliographical material at the end of each chapter was designed for further reading about "the ladies." It does not include all of the research collected by the author. The book is not an academic project. It was written over a twenty year period to give readers an overview of the lives of these fascinating women and to encourage more in-depth reading about them from sources most easily obtainable.

Contents

                                                                  Page

Introduction

		Page
Part I.	**Pocahontas.** c. 1596–1617. The savior of the first English colony, Jamestown, Virginia.	**1**
Part II.	**Lucy Terry Prince.** c. 1730-1821. The first woman to practice before the Supreme Court of the United States in Circuit and win her case.	**23**
Part III.	**Mary Edwards Walker.** c. 1832-1919. The first and only woman to be awarded the Congressional Medal of Honor.	**35**
Part IV.	**Sarah Josepha Hale.** c. 1788-1879. The editor of *Godey's* who gave us Thanksgiving Day.	**59**
Part V.	**Victoria Claflin Woodhull.** c. 1838-1927. The first woman to run for the presidency of the United States—five times.	**73**

THANK YOU

Linda Baker Tippet, librarian, El Centro Community College, Dallas, Texas.

Beverly Holmes, former library director, El Centro Community College, Dallas, Texas.

Carolyn Thorne, librarian, technical services center, Dallas County Community College District.

James Cole, former Chief of Staff to Congressman Ralph Hall, Rockwall, Texas.

Mary Cecil, publisher, editor, writer of *The Rockwall Chronicle*, manuscript copyreader, typist, and mother of my Godchild, Meg.

David Wilfong, cover

Hallie Garner, book preparation

for

discovering manuscripts
finding books out of print
taking photographs under difficult circumstances
enjoying the search for these extraordinary women

Part I

POCAHONTAS

"And the Lord said unto her, nations are in thy womb, and two manner of people shall be separated from thy bowels; and one people shall be stronger than the other people and the other shall serve the younger."
                    Genesis, Chapter 25:23

Women Short-Changed by History

Pocahontas

At least a million people in the United States claim to be and may be descendants of Pocahontas. Some of them look like Native Americans of the Pamunkey tribe; others are blond, blue-eyed, skinny, round, short, long-nosed, snub-nosed, all proud to have sprung from the loins of the Indian maiden and her husband John Rolfe, a sturdy English squire. He was her second choice for a mate. Her first choice was Captain John Smith, of questionable character, a soldier of fortune, a lover of women and a man who knew how to survive in the ever-expanding world of the seventeenth century.

Few accounts of the first meeting of Pocahontas and Smith exist, except in his **Generall Historie of Virginia**. She left no written record during her brief life. Smith left several accounts which seemed to improve with writing, not mentioning Pocahontas in his first general history, but in the third retelling of his story and of how she saved his life and the Jamestown Colony.

John Rolfe had to plead with the royal governor for permission to marry Pocahontas who was an Indian princess while he was but a commoner. Disclaiming the desire of "Carnall affection" in his letter to Governor Thomas Dale, but for reasons of his own salvation and for the good of the plantation, God and country, Rolfe asked for Pocahontas. He was "in love" with her according to contemporaries, but was she "in love" with him? He endured "strange and violent passions" to her "mild affection" for him. Was the memory of her first love a motivating factor for marriage to an Englishman who would take her to his country, Smith's country, too?

In Arlington National Cemetery there is a six foot stone grave marker listing the first families of Virginia. This is to the memory of Thomas Rolfe, the only child of the union of Pocahontas and John Rolfe. The remains of Pocahontas lie somewhere underneath the Parish Church of St. George at Gravesend in Kent, England. They have never been returned to her homeland because the stone under which she was interred in the chancel floor was not marked. The church burned and was rebuilt without finding any evidence of her remains.

Anxious to sail for Virginia in 1617, Rolfe, now secretary and Recorder-General of the Virginia Company, and Captain Argall, who had bought Pocahontas for a copper kettle and had carried her as a hostage to Jamestown, waited for the fog to lift. There is an impression that her death and burial on the eve of the returning expedition to the colony was a hurried, inconvenient occurrence. At Plymouth, Thomas Rolfe, the sickly two year son, was left in the care of Sir Lewis Stukely until his uncle Henry Rolfe, a London merchant, could retrieve him.

John Rolfe never saw his son again. He died a week before the 1622 Indian massacre of Jamestown which almost destroyed the colony and ended "the peace of Pocahontas." Eventually, Thomas returned to Virginia, made a brief visit to his Indian relatives and joined the militia which wiped out the remains of his grandfather Powhatan's Confederacy.

She had heard rumors of the arrival in the bay of winged sailing ships. From the tribal council of great chief Powhatan came word of men with pale skins covered with strange chest and leg coverings who were invading the territory of the Algonquian-speaking tribes in the Chesapeake area.

This April morning, Pocahontas was hiding in the marsh grass along the James River. Without telling anyone, she had come to see for herself what was happening on the river. The child watched the men in the small ships as they called out directions to each other in their preparations to land. Her attention was focused on one individual who seemed to stand alone on the deck of the lead ship, gazing at the shore, deferring to no one on board. He was bearded, had slightly waving brown hair, was probably in his late twenties and had a decidedly arrogant stance. His appearance was fascinating to Pocahontas. She could not know that he had been imprisoned for thirteen weeks for mutinous behavior and had just been released from below decks. For Pocahontas, he represented another world that she wanted to know. And he was handsome with his pale skin and his brown, curling hair.

Curious by nature, adventurous, playful (as her tribal name, Matoaka, implied), spoiled by a doting father unable to deny her anything, Pocahontas had traveled alone through the forest to see the strangers. Would the ancient prophesy of the destruction of her people be fulfilled by them?

Powhatan had advised his council in watchful waiting to see if these men were exploring, intent on trade or planning to stay. Any attempt at settlement would be dealt with immediately. The Jamestown settlers, arriving that morning in 1607 in their three ships, were under constant surveillance by different tribes of the Powhatan confederacy. Trade was acceptable to the Indians, settlement was not.

Pocahontas returned to the Indian court at Werowocomoco, silent and observing, comparing her father and the Englishman she had seen on the river.

The Englishmen came ashore and began building a flimsy stockade around their encampment. It did not prevent the Indians from attacking the camp nor from killing the men who strayed outside the barricades looking for food. Because Jamestown was set in a malarial swamp along the river, disease struck immediately. Poor judgement and desertion among the handful of survivors of the first year, 1608, forced Captain John Smith to take over acquisition of a food supply. He had been elevated to a governing council position because many of the "better quality" men had died, although he had initially been selected for the council by the investors in the Virginia Company.

The investors had ignored his lack of family name and status in English society because they needed a resourceful representative with experience in warfare and survival. According to Smith, at the age of fifteen or sixteen, he had been a mercenary in the continuing battles between Christians in eastern Europe and Moslems. Taken in battle by the Turks, he wrote that he was sold into slavery, but he beat out the "braines" of his owner and escaped, wandering the steppes until he found a caravan route. He crossed Poland, Hungary, Bavaria, France; then to Gibraltar, Tangier and the Barbary coast. He finally returned to England at the age of twenty-four, a veteran, eager for more adventuring. In many of his escapades, "ladies" featured prominently. Whether this was to ensure readers for his books or because of a "way with women," he was daring, charming and certainly resourceful.

In bargaining for corn, he would have to locate the camp of a tribal chief and present himself as a leader and negotiator for the foreigners. Smith had heard of the great Powhatan through the coastal Indians. He was eager to explore the land and rivers. The expedition was perfect for his talents.

It was on this journey to Werowocomoco, the court of Powhatan, that he would be taken captive by Opechancanough, brother of Powhatan and implacable foe of the English. But, Opechancanough observed the protocols of war and was prepared to grant Smith certain formalities before killing him. Although Smith was paraded through Indian villages to see if he was the tall, vicious white man, perpetrator of atrocities against the Indians, it was obvious that the shorter, stockier Englishman in his breastplate and thigh plates was not the guilty person.

In January, 1608, Smith was finally brought to the longhouse of the "awesome" Powhatan where he would forever become linked to Pocahontas and she to him. The history of the Jamestown colony and of the English in America was changed by the fascination and love the Indian princess would bestow upon Captain John Smith.

Only one eye witness recorded their meeting in Werowocomoco. Smith, himself, described what happened to him in his 1624 manuscript, *The General Historie of Virginia, New England and the Summer Isles.* After Smith was brought into the camp, he was feasted. Then began a powwow, probably to decide what to do with the important prisoner.

Powhatan ordered two great stones to be placed upon the ground. Smith was dragged to them and his head placed firmly between them. Smith believed the Indians would "beate out his braines." Suddenly, it was Pocahontas, "the King's dearest daughter . . .got his head in her armes and laid her owne upon his to save him from death . . . "

Was he rescued from death by Pocahontas or was he participating in a ritual which had a different meaning to the Princess and her tribe? When she covered his body with hers to save him from the war clubs of Powhatan, was it a symbolic gesture of betrothal, obligation, tribal acceptance, adoption or all of these? Smith never knew. And, he probably did not consider any possibility except that his life was spared. However, the results of this encounter were immediate. Smith was returned to Jamestown with "twelve guides" who were responsible for his safety.

But, in Jamestown, all was confusion. The leaders were talking of abandoning the starving colony. The arrival of Smith and the Indians was a complete surprise and certainly forestalled the decision to leave.

Even as Powhatan's warriors arrived in Jamestown to obtain two great guns and a grindstone to bind the friendship between himself and Smith, Pocahontas was preparing relief for the colonists.

"Now every once in three or four days, Pocahontas, with her attendants, brought *him* (italic mine) so much provision that it saved many of their lives, that else for all this had starved with hunger." Turkey, deer, cornbread, and raccoons were all part of the provisions for Jamestown.

Smith commented on the bounty of Powhatan "to revive their dead spirits." He included in this supply "especially the love of Pocahontas." Of course, he must have known for whom that love existed. He probably considered it to be a child's affection for this older man of twenty-eight.

In the early spring, when Pocahontas first came to the fort she could not have been older than eleven or twelve because she wore nothing. William Strachey called her "wanton" because she proceeded to do handsprings down the streets of Jamestown with the young cabin boys following her, laughing and attempting to imitate her antics. Smith had studied the Pamunkey customs and he was unconcerned. He knew that after puberty, women wore decorated leather aprons around their middles. Pocahontas was a child, not yet of marriageable age when she played in the streets of Jamestown. She was merely fun-loving, true to her tribal name Matoaka.

But, within six months, the status of Pocahontas changed. She took on the role of ambassador for Powhatan who sent her to gain the release of seven Indian hostages. Smith wrote that he delivered them to Pocahontas "for whose sake" he gave them liberty. He also needed to keep on friendly terms with Powhatan. He had been ordered by the Jamestown council to return to Werowocomoco and invite Powhatan to Jamestown to be crowned King by the Crown's emissary. This would make Powhatan subservient to the English King. Smith knew that Powhatan understood the implications of the proposal and he was reluctant to go on what he thought was a foolish attempt to keep the Indian ruler from attacking Jamestown.

When Smith reached the Indian village, Powhatan was not there. It was time for the October harvest festival and the women were in charge. Smith and the Englishmen with him were invited to stay for the festivities. Pocahontas and the Pamunkey maidens also could have been performing a final acknowledgement of the coming of age.

Dancing naked out of woods, "covered behind and before with a few green leaves," wearing antlers on her head and otter skins at her waist, Pocahontas joined thirty other singing, howling maidens in a display "with most *excellent* ill varieties," whatever those may have been.

When these excellent ill varieties were over, and the paint and greenery removed, Smith was invited to lodgings where he was accosted by the "Nymphs" crying, "Love you not me? Love you not me?" Did he or didn't he? What was an English gentleman or a soldier of fortune to do? Pocahontas was obviously no longer a child, but a woman taking part in the tribe's harvest fertility festival.

A feast was prepared while the "maidens" danced and sang around Smith and the five other Englishmen with him. When the feasting ended, "they conducted him to his lodging." And no more was said by Smith of the action as night covered the Englishmen and the Indian women.

"The next day came Powhatan."

The great chief of the Powhatan Confederacy did not trust the English. By this time Powhatan and his brother, Opechancanough, wanted them to sail away and never return. When Smith urged the chief to go to Jamestown to be crowned "Emperour," he refused. He did not want a copper crown, a coronation robe nor a position of vassalage to the English sovereign. Another round trip to Jamestown was made by Smith and Captain Newport, who was temporarily in charge of negotiations. Two of the four remaining councillors had drowned, and they were needed in Jamestown.

When they returned to Werowocamoco, the coronation there proved to be a disaster. Powhatan would not kneel and refused to wear the crown. He reacted by moving his court further into the forest where the English could not find him. He also decided to kill Smith, hoping this would encourage the departure of all the English from confederacy lands.

Pocahontas either overheard the plot to kill Smith or was told of it indirectly. It was to be accomplished while the English were still in the Indian village, finishing the evening meal, after the departure of Powhatan. It began raining heavily and Smith decided to spend the night in the village. Pocahontas found him there after traveling through the forest at night at the height of the storm.

When Pocahontas found Smith, he gratefully offered her a handful of trinkets for warning him. For her it was almost an insult: trinkets for a life that she had ritualistically sworn to protect. Smith said she cried. Why wouldn't she cry? She saved his life at the risk of her own and he offered her trinkets in return.

Smith immediately left the Indian town by shallow boat, not for Jamestown but to find corn desperately needed by the Jamestown colony. A messenger from Jamestown looking for Smith was also saved by Pocahontas when she hid him from the wrath of Powhatan, then sent him on his way to Smith.

Finally, returning to Jamestown without food, Smith knew that desperate measures must be taken to save the colony, and he made his decision, "he that will not worke shall not eate." The colony teetered on the brink of extinction as the third supply of new colonists arrived. But, they were in no better condition than the Jamestown survivors. Sick, hungry, injured from storms at sea, the newcomers arrived to take part in a power struggle that several factions hoped would evict Smith of his authority.

Then, a terrible accident happened. A spark ignited Smith's powder keg while he was on the river. The explosion "tore the flesh from his body and thigh." The pain was so excruciating that he jumped from the boat into the cold river water to escape the burning flesh; he almost drowned. Even in this condition, his enemies in Jamestown, determined to take control, plotted to assassinate him.

He was forced to return to England for treatment, leaving the aristocratic bureaucracy of the Virginia company to fight among itself. Pocahontas knew nothing of Smith's troubles and he did not leave a message for her when he left. His condition was critical as he was carried aboard the *Falcon* in September, 1609 and the ships of the Third Supply began the journey back to England

Smith, in time, recovered and returned to the New World to explore the Massachusetts area, the future home of Pilgrims and Puritans, but he never again set foot in Jamestown. Neither did Pocahontas *of her own free will*. She believed Smith was dead as all rumors indicated after the gunpowder explosion. It was not until she was taken hostage and returned to Jamestown that she learned Smith was alive, although she never spoke of her feelings to anyone.

The Jamestown colony floundered and starved during the terrible winter of 1609-10. Cannibalism was reported by George Percy, president of the council after Smith, and the charge was repeated by Smith in his *Historie*. Powhatan was implacable and determined by boycott and terror to force the English to leave. The English reciprocated with atrocities against Indian women and children. Pocahontas' visits had ceased with the departure of Smith. She was no longer with her father but had gone to live with distant relatives, the Patawamakes, possibly because of an estrangement with her father over her close ties to the English. William Strachey reported that she was now married to a Captain Kocoun "some two years synce." But,

Strachey, who also wrote a *Historie* in 1612, has the only reference to this marriage and Pocahontas never referred to it.

When she disappeared into the country of the Patawamakes, she did one more favor for the English. A young reprobate, Henry Spellman, serving as an English hostage, ran away from Powhatan's camp. Pocahontas found him lost in the forest, and he said that she guided him to the Patawamakes where he found refuge.

Just as the colonists could stand no more of starvation and once again prepared to abandon the colony, Sir Thomas Dale arrived. Deputy Governor Dale had been named Marshal of Virginia. A military man and a strict disciplinarian, he had been recommended for the job by the King to bring the Virginia Company to heel and make it a paying concern. To force the colonists to stay and work, he ordered that any attempt to escape from Jamestown meant either hanging or being broken on the rack. For stealing from the small store of food, a colonist could be bound to a tree with a dagger stuck through his tongue until he starved to death. Dale was determined that these settlers should return a profit to King and company. The war of attrition with the Indians was another matter. How could he force them into some kind of peace?

Captain Samuel Argall, a future governor of the colony, and in 1613 a provider of corn for Jamestown discovered the leverage in Powhatan's favorite daughter Pocahontas. She was still with the Patawamake's werowance Japazaws and his wife.

Argall went to Japazaws with a proposition. Wouldn't his wife like to own a gleaming copper kettle and perhaps a few other trinkets in exchange for Pocahontas? His wife was edgy about the trade, but Japazaws saw a future in trade with a powerful Englishman, so they plotted the kidnapping of Pocahontas. On the pretext of showing her the boat, because of her interest in everything English, she was lured aboard, locked in a storeroom while the copper pot was handed to Japazaws' wife. Argall had promised that he would not hurt her, but would merely "keepe her till they could conclude a peace treaty."

Did she fight, protest, try to jump overboard? Only men at the time wrote about the capture of Pocahontas. Since then, only Frances Mossiker has written of Pocahontas from a woman's point of view.

What did Pocahontas think about forcibly being returned to Jamestown as a hostage after a five year absence? Most of the people she had known and befriended had returned to England or were dead. Had she learned of Captain Smith's survival? A ransom note was sent to her father stating she would be returned to him after Powhatan gave back "our men, swordes, pieces and tooles . . ." and plenty of corn.

Pocahontas was now seventeen or eighteen and was of marriageable age. By all accounts she was attractive. What could the English do with their hostage? Christianize her; teach her English or possibly marry her off. Philip Barbour suggested his book, *Pocahontas and Her World,* as do several other male historians, that Pocahontas trusted the English enough to make no attempt to escape and to live with them.

She was initially placed under the tutelage of the Reverend Alexander Whitaker by Sir Thomas Dale. These two men, later with John Rolfe, would initiate her into English culture. The first thing to do was to dress her properly in a high-necked gown, whale bone corset and shoes instead of the small, fringed apron of the mature Indian woman. No more would she be called Matoaka or Pocahontas, but by her baptismal name Rebecca.

John Rolfe was a neighbor of Reverend Whitaker of Rock Hall in Henrico Parish, where Rolfe was said to have conducted his experiments in the cultivation of tobacco. Thanks to Rolfe, the tobacco industry would flourish and become the economic base of Jamestown, causing the colony to prosper for the first time. Tobacco led Rolfe up the James River and Bible study with Reverend Whitaker brought him into contact with Pocahontas.

Sometime in 1613, Rolfe fell in love with Pocahontas. In a letter to Governor Thomas Dale, Rolfe describes the "passions of my troubled soul." At some length Rolfe wrote of his attempts to deal with his feelings toward Pocahontas. It is not "my hungrye appetite" but for the good of the plantation, the honor of the country, the glory of God and his own salvation that Rolfe appealed to Dale.

What did Pocahontas, Lady Rebecca after baptism, think of all that happened to her since the initial contact with the English? What could a kidnapped, captive Indian princess have thought about her future? Did she have any choices? Englishmen in Jamestown, who later wrote accounts of the courting of Pocahontas, told of John Rolfe and his feelings, but no one asked Pocahontas what she wanted to do. She had no intimates among the few women in the colony and no one set down anything she said about Rolfe.

Ralph Harmon, the son of an investor in the company and sometimes acting clerk of the colony, was in Virginia when Pocahontas was taken hostage, christened and married to John Rolfe. He writes in his *True Discourse* that her kidnapping was to encourage Powhatan to return English captives. He wrote that Rolfe was "worthy of much commendations . . . witness his marriage to Powhatan's daughter *merely for the good and honor of the plantation.*" (Italics mine.)

Governor Dale finally permitted Pocahontas to visit her father in 1614. Rolfe went with her up the Pamunkey River. No offer had come from Powhatan to ransom his daughter whom Dale wrote "had been long a prisoner with us."

Powhatan never appeared.

Pocahontas was sent ashore to mingle and speak to tribal members, but she remained aloof and waited for a message from her father. None came. Finally, after the group returned to Jamestown, Powhatan sent word to Governor Dale that "his daughter should be my child, and ever dwell with me." It would seem that everyone was satisfied with the arrangement. They would all now live in peace and be happy, but still no one spoke for Pocahontas. She was the pawn. First, she had saved Jamestown by preventing mass starvation; now she was the instrument for securing a peace which would enable the English colony to expand and prosper. This period, beginning with her kidnapping by Argall, and ending with her death, became known as the Peace of Pocahontas. While she lived, there was peace.

The Church of England ceremony uniting Lady Rebecca and John Rolfe took place in Jamestown. Her father did not give the bride away but sent "an older uncle of hers" to give her in marriage and two of his sons to act as witnesses.

Did Mr. and Mrs. Rolfe live happily ever after? Several Englishmen, including John Smith described "affection," "civility," and "harmony," but never passion. Pocahontas had been well-trained as an English wife in Reverend Whitaker's house. She knew her place in society. She studied industriously to speak English well and committed herself to Christianity and to the Church of England, abandoning her previous beliefs or so it was written. For Rolfe, it was certainly a marriage of convenience. He, like John Smith earlier, was accused of "social climbing and marrying above his position."

In the spring of 1615 Thomas Rolfe was born with women of his mother's tribe in attendance at her request.

The peace was holding. Tobacco was a cash crop in England and it was time to promote the Virginia Colony in London with mother, husband and child, the first legitimate union between Indian and English, and the only recorded marriage for more than two centuries.

After hearing Harmon's news that "Pocahontas is generally reported to be his (Rolfe's) delight and darling," Governor Dale sent Harmon back to Powhatan. Dale asked Harmon to "procure a daughter of his" (Powhatan's) whom he "would gladly make his nearest companion, wife and bedfellow." Of course, Dale already had a wife in England. Powhatan replied that the English had one of his daughters and that was enough. He probably knew of Dale's previous marriage.

When Dale returned to England in 1616, he took the Rolfes with him "to advance the good of the plantation," which was virtually bankrupt and needed all the help it could get to renew interest in the enterprise. Dale hoped that Pocahontas, converted, baptized, certainly distinctive in appearance, speaking English with an unusual, exotic voice could do that.

John Chamberlain wrote to his friend Dudley Carleton that "Sir Thomas Dale is arrived from Virginia (bringing Indians—10 or 12) among whom the most remarkable is Pocahontas, daughter of Powhatan." Then he added, rather cryptically, "There is no profit to be expected."

An official of the company made the arrangements for Pocahontas and her child at one of the oldest inns in London, the Belle Sauvage. Whether it was the appropriateness of the name or the limited expense account of the company, the rowdy, roisterous tavern must have been a shock to Pocahontas. But it was from here that she went forth to be received by James I and his wife, Queen Anne.

Captain John Smith had written to the Queen before the presentation of Pocahontas at court. He described how "she hazarded the beating out of her own brains to save mine;" and "she . . . was still the instrument to preserve this Colonie from death." He beseeched the Queen to do her some honor. However, he did not appear to greet her. Smith said that he was busy preparing to sail to New England on a voyage of settlement. There may have been another reason for not meeting Pocahontas, a dislike or jealousy of Rolfe who had married Lady Rebecca. Perhaps more important, the guilt he must have felt for leaving Jamestown after his accident without leaving a message for Pocahontas, or writing to her from England after his injuries had healed. This was the child/woman who had saved his life.

His letter to the Queen could have been an attempt to make amends for this lack of consideration. Conversely, Pocahontas was almost eager to get to England. She had learned her lessons well in language, dress, and deportment. Perhaps it was Smith she wanted to see and impress.

At the English court, Pocahontas was well received—why wouldn't she have been? The savior of the English Colony, an Indian princess of royal bearing must have impressed Queen Anne. The queen and her court loved games and divertissements and the Matoaka (playful one)

Pocahontas

in Pocahontas caused her to be "frequently admitted to wait on her Majesty." Robert Beverley wrote about the introduction of Pocahontas to the court by Lady de la Warre, after which she was invited to "Plays, Balls and other publick Entertainments . . . " John Rolfe was not so fortunate. "Poor Gentleman," said Beverley, "her husband called to account for marrying a Princess Royal without the King's Consent." He was not invited to many of the festivities. Nor was he given any allowance to supplement the four pounds a week that the company gave for the maintenance of Pocahontas and her son. Even his experiments in tobacco which made him the "father of the Virginia tobacco industry" were held against him. King James I hated tobacco and disdained people who smoked "the filthy weed." At the most exciting, extravagant festivity of the year, the Twelfth Night Masque, John Rolfe did not sit near his wife who was a special guest of the monarchs. He was relegated to a balcony and ignored. He was, indeed, a "Poor Gentleman."

Pocahontas was the sensation of London society and male contemporaries writing about her time at court all said she enjoyed herself.

But the climate of London society began changing for the Rolfes. John Chamberlain, who wrote of "the most remarkable person is Pocahontas" when she first arrived in England in June 1616, wrote another letter to his friend Dudley Carleton in February 1617. "Here is a fine picture of no fair lady. And yet with her tricking up and high style and titles, you might think her and her worshipful husband to be somebody, if you do not know that the poor company of Virginia, out of their poverty, are fain to allow her four pound a week for her maintenance."

Then Pocahontas became ill. The pollution of London, the smell of smoke and open sewers, the fog and dampness permeated the air. The Indian band, who had greeted the sun in the river and had cast tobacco on the clear waters as a gift to God could not breath in London air or swim in the Thames. The Rolfes moved to Brentfort up the Thames where there were trees, fresh air, room for Thomas to run and play and a quietude not to be had at the Belle Sauvage Tavern.

It was here at Brentfort that Captain John Smith finally came to pay his respects to Lady Rebecca Rolfe.

His excuse for not appearing sooner, he said, was his absence from London on pressing matters having to do with the Plymouth Company, trying to put together a deal to colonize in New England. He arrived unannounced at Brentfort with a few friends. His greeting from Pocahontas was not what he had expected. Overcome with emotion, she turned her back on the group and disappeared for "two or three houres." Smith in his *Historie* indicates that he was embarrassed by her silence and subsequent disappearance.

When she returned to face Smith, one of the last statements she made to him was, "They did tell us alwaies you were dead, and I knew no other till I came to Plimoth." Did Pocahontas mean that she would not have married Rolfe if she had known Smith was alive? Did she believe that the adoption ritual was also an engagement and a pledge for life?

This was the only meeting of Pocahontas and Captain John Smith in England. It was the last time they would speak together. It was obvious that her health was declining after the New Year in the "perpetual weeping weather" that seemed to bring sickness and fever to England as well as western Europe. The Indians were and are susceptible to upper respiratory ailments and the weather aggravated their health problems. She could have contracted tuberculosis or pneumonia.

Pocahontas was very reluctant to leave England, but her husband had just been appointed Secretary and Recorder-General of Virginia. He could not wait to return to his tobacco fields in his new position of importance. But, he did not tell his wife immediately of his promotion and the necessity of returning to Jamestown. She did not want to go, whether because of her sickness or because of Smith. Barbour says the men and their wives of the Virginia company were always "aloof" from the princess. She considered herself friendless and was returning to Jamestown "sore against her will."

Ignoring her sickness and depression, Pocahontas and her little son, Thomas, were carried aboard the *George*, flagship of the returning fleet. In charge and newly elected Deputy Governor of Virginia was Admiral Samuel Argall, the venal and overbearing Englishman who had plotted the kidnapping of Pocahontas four years earlier. Now, he watched as the Rolfes boarded his flagship with the surviving tribal members. London's pollution was too much for the Pamunkeys. Several died; even little Thomas was ill.

The fleet sailed downriver from London to the town of Gravesend. There it was forced to put in to take Pocahontas ashore. She had become too sick to continue the voyage.

"The Virginia woman whose picture I sent you died this last week at Gravesend . . . " reported John Chamberlain in a letter to his friend, Dudley Carleton. Pocahontas had known she was dying and was stoic and accepting of the fact.

She was quickly buried beneath chancel floor in the Church of St. George on March 31, 1617. There was no time to provide for an inscription above her. Her name is misspelled in the Burial Register and on the commemorative stone. Her husband's name was John, not Thomas: "March 21 - Rebecca Wrolfe wyffe of Thomas Wrolfe gent. A Virginia Lady borne was buried in the Chauncel" — three lines in the Burial Register.

The fleet was waiting; the winds were favorable and on the tide the ships of the company set sail for Virginia. Her little boy remained behind; he did not see his father again. John Rolfe returned to Virginia and remarried within a year.

The ancient church at Gravesend burned in 1727, and was rebuilt without searching for the remains of Pocahontas. Not until the twentieth century did anyone seriously consider identifying her burial site. Too much time had passed—her memory too long neglected. The second St. George Church was almost demolished because its parishioners moved away and it became run-down. But, donations and subscriptions from her land and from her adopted country saved the building. Today it is the Anglo-American Chapel of Unity, dedicated to the memory of Pocahontas. In the chapel garden, there is a commemorative plaque:

THIS STONE COMMEMORATES
Princess Pocahontas or Metoaka
Daughter of
The Mighty Indian Chief Powhatan

GENTLE AND HUMANE, SHE WAS THE FRIEND OF THE EARLIEST STRUGGLING ENGLISH COLONISTS WHOM SHE BOLDLY RESCUED, PROTECTED, AND HELPED.
ON HER CONVERSION TO CHRISTIANITY IN 1613, SHE RECEIVED IN BAPTISM THE NAME REBECCA, AND SHORTLY AFTERWARDS BECAME THE WIFE OF THOMAS ROLFE, A SETTLER IN VIRGINIA. SHE VISITED ENGLAND WITH HER HUSBAND IN 1616, WAS GRACIOUSLY RECEIVED BY QUEEN ANNE WIFE OF JAMES I. IN THE TWENTY-SECOND YEAR OF HER AGE DIED AT GRAVESEND, WHILE PREPARING TO REVISIT HER NATIVE COUNTRY, AND WAS BURIED NEAR THIS SPOT ON MARCH 21st, 1617.

More poignant to the Gravesend pilgrim are the redbud trees from Virginia that blossom in the spring rains of Kent. The garden is a lovely place. And, Pocahontas is far from home.

Selected Bibliography

Smith, John. *The General Historie of Virginia, New England, and the Summer Isles.* London, 1624. March of America Facsimile Series, No. 18, University Microfilms, Inc. 1966. Especially Books III and IV. These books introduced Pocahontas to the English-reading world. The reader must judge the veracity of the accounts.

The following four books contain accounts of Pocahontas by men who were her contemporaries:

Strachey, William, gent. *The Historie of Travel into Virginia Britania (1612).* Louis B. Wright, Virginia Freund, editors. London: Printed for the Hakluyt Society, 1953.

Chamberlain, John. *The Chamberlain Letters.* Elizabeth McClure Thomson, editor. New York: G. P. Putnam's Sons, 1965.

Beverley, Robert. *The History and Present State of Virginia.* Louis B. Wright, editor. Chapel Hill, NC: University of North Carolina Press, 1947.

Harmor, Ralph. *A True Discourse of the Present State of Virginia.* Reprinted from the London edition of 1615. Richmond, VA: Virginia State Library, 1957. Introduction by A. L. Rouse. The Letter from John Rolfe to Governor Thomas Dale requesting the hand of Pocahontas is reprinted at the end of the book. It is an amazing document.

Barbour, Philip L. *Pocahontas and Her World.* Boston: Houghton Mifflin Co., 1970.

Mossiker, Frances. *Pocahontas the Life and the Legend.* New York: Alfred A. Knopf, 1976.

Robertson, Wyndham and R. A .Brock. *Pocahontas, alias Matoaka, and her Descendants.* Baltimore, MD: Southern Book Company, 1956.

Stith, William. *History of the First Discovery and Settlement of Virginia.* Williamsburg, 1747. Reprinted by University of North Carolina Press, Chapel Hill, NC, 1912.

Women Short-Changed by History

Part II

LUCY TERRY PRINCE

"I will follow my heart and it will lead me home."
Anonymous

Women Short-Changed by History

Governor and Council—June 1785.

SATURDAY, 4th June 1785.

Met according to Adjournment.
Present the Members attending yesterday,—There not being a Quorum Adjourned to 9 o'Clock Monday next.

MONDAY, June 6th 1785.

Met according to Adjournment.
Present. His Excellency, Thomas Chittenden Esqr. His Honor Paul Spooner, Esqr. The Honble Moses Robinson Peter Olcott Benjamin Emmons Thomas Moredock Ira Allen & John Throop Esquires.

There being no Secretary present Resolved that Mr. Daniel Buck, be and he is hereby appointed Secy. P. T. who was accordingly duly Sworn to the faithfull discharge of said office.

Resolved that, the Honble Peter Olcott & Ira Allen Esquires be a Committee to join a Committee from the General Assembly on the Petition of the Inhabitants of More Town, [Bradford,] to State facts and make Report thereon.

Resolved that the Honble Moses Robinson Esqr. be a Committee to join a Committee from the General Assembly on the Memorial of William Marsh, praying the appointment of a committee to Examine into the Circumstances concerning a Certain Note, to state facts to the General Assembly at their Next Session.

An Act entitled an Act to authenticate the Deeds therein Mentioned was Recd. Read and approved.

Resolved that Jesse Cook of Willmington be and he is hereby appointed a Justice of the Peace in and for the County of Windham; And that the Clerk of the County Court, be & he is hereby directed to Enter his name in the Commission of the peace in his office.

[Reso]lved that Benjamin Olds Esqr. of Marlborough in the County of [Windha]m be and he is hereby appointed a Justice of the peace in & for [the Coun]ty of Windham; And that the Clerk of the County Court be [he]reby directed to Enter his name in the Commission of the [peace in h]is office.

[Adjourn]ed to 8 o'Clock Tomorrow.

TUESDAY, June 7th 1785.

Met according to Adjournment.
Present His Excellency Thomas Chittenden Esqr. His Honor Paul Spooner Esqr. The Honble Moses Robinson Esqr. Peter Olcott Benjamin Emmons Thomas Moredock John Throop & Ira Allen Esqrs.

On the Representation of Lucy Prince, wife of Abijah Prince, and others shewing that, the said Abijah, Lucy and Family, are greatly oppressed & injured by John and Ormas Noyce, in the possession and enjoyment of a certain farm or Piece of Land, on which the said Abijah and Lucy now Lives, the Council having Taken the same into consideration and made due enquiry, are of Opinion that the said Abijah and Lucy are much injured, and that unless the Town Take some due Methods to protect said Abijah, Lucy & family in the enjoyment of their possession, they must soon unavoidably fall upon the Charity of the Town.

Therefore Resolved that His Excellency be Requested to write to the Selectmen of the Town of Guilford Recommending to them to Take some effectual Measures to protect the said Abijah, Lucy & family, in the Possession of said Lands until the said dispute can be equally & equitably settled.

Record of Governor and Council Meeting of June 7, 1785 recommending that they "take some effectual Measure to protect the said Abijah, Lucy & family."

Lucy Terry Prince

P*rimary* sources on the life of Lucy Terry Prince are limited to a poem, an harassment case in **Records of the Governor and Council, State of Vermont, Vol. III**, the recollections of several lawyers, and some legal papers concerning taxes and property in her husband's name. Her most significant contribution to "women's" history, a court case which she pleaded before the Circuit Court with Supreme Court Justice Samuel Chase presiding, is not to be found in the **Federal Digest**, nor in **Federal Cases**, Circuit and District Courts. This courtroom drama has been pieced together in a fictionalized biography by Bernard and Jonathan Katz. There are also hints of the strong woman behind the story in **Negro Slavery in Old Deerfield** by George Sheldon. The oral tradition of her participation in the trial was handed down several generations by relatives and friends.

Born in Africa, kidnapped and sold into slavery, Lucy was purchased by Ebenezer Wells, baptized and educated by him. After her marriage to Abijah Prince, who bought her freedom from Wells, Lucy became an active participant in community affairs and never doubted her right to defend her property and to insist on justice for herself and for her family.

Women Short-Changed by History

Lucy Terry Prince

If Lucy could recall her life in Africa before she was kidnapped and sold to Ebenezer Wells in Rhode Island, she never spoke of it, although it was said of her that she was a great story teller and children constantly filled her home begging for tales.

When Wells brought her home to Deerfield, Massachusetts at the age of five or six, he had her baptized and began to teach her to read and write. It is unfortunate that most of her poems and stories, written while she lived with the Wells family, were not set down or were lost. The single poem that has survived is not great literature, but it sheds some light on what was happening during the French and Indian War along the Massachusetts frontier:

> August 'twas the twenty-fifth,
> Seventeen hundred forty-six;
> The Indians did in ambush lay.
> Some very valient men to slay,
> The names of whom I'll not leave out.
> Samuel Allen like a hero fout,
> And though he was so brave and bold,
> His face no more shall we behold.
> Eleazer Hawks was killed outright,
> Before he had time to fight,
> Before he did the Indians see,
> Was shot and killed immediately.

Oliver Amsden he was slain,
Which caused his friends much grief and pain.
Simeon Amsden they found dead,
Not many rods distant from his head.
Adonijah Gillett we do hear
Did lose his life which was so dear.
John Sadler fled across the water,
And thus escaped the dreadful slaughter.
Eunice Allen see the Indians coming,
And hopes to save herself by running,
And had not her petticoats stopped her,
The awful creatures had not catched her,
Nor tommy hawked her on her head,
And left her on the ground for dead.
Young Samuel Allen, Oh lack-a-day!
Was taken and carried to Canada.

Bars Fight, written by Lucy in 1746, is a narrative of an Abenaki massacre in a meadow (bars) near Sam Dickenson's farm adjoining Deerfield. The poem was not published until 1855, thirty years after Lucy's death. It was probably remembered as a ballad in the oral tradition. Her reputation for "wit and wisdom" could not have been based upon one poem, but it did secure her place in African American literature. Her reputation in history is more substantial, although it is based on stories by people who knew and respected her and on two court cases.

Her appearances before the Governor's Council of Vermont and before Supreme Court Judge Samuel Chase would be in defense of her husband Abijah Prince's property during and after his lifetime. He was the great love of her life.

Prince had been the property of the Reverend Benjamin Doolittle, who emancipated Prince on or before his death and also left him property in Northfield, Massachusetts on which Prince paid taxes. After

Doolittle's death, he became "the servant" of Ebenezer Wells, who also "owned" Lucy. This "free man of substance" was considerably older than Lucy when they first met in Wells' home. Abijah was born in Wallenford, Massachusetts in 1706. He courted Lucy for several years because it may have taken that long to pay Wells for Lucy. The couple was married in the Wells' home by a justice of the peace in 1756 when Lucy was twenty-six and Abijah was fifty.

By 1764 they were living in Guilford, Vermont where Abijah had been given property by Samuel Field "for services rendered." He also owned the property in Northfield near 'Bijah's Brook and in Sunderland, Vermont not far from the home of Ethan Allen, a revolutionary war hero. The Sunderland property may have been received because of Bijah's participation in the French and Indian War, serving in the Deerfield militia.

Abijah and Lucy Bijah were obviously a well-to-do "free" couple who entertained in their home and gathered together blacks and whites in evenings of intellectual stimulation and entertainment.

Their first-born son was Caesar. Then, the names became more creative: Durexa, Drucella, Festus, Tatnai and, lastly, Abijah, Jr. All of the children were educated in Guilford schools. Lucy hoped that one of her sons would go on to the Free School which later would become Williams College. Although there is no record of her application to the Free School, George Sheldon in "Negro History in Old Deerfield" gives an account of her three hour plea for admission before the trustees quoting law and gospel. Which son was turned down? No name is given, but it may have been the fun-loving Festus.

Festus and Caesar enlisted in the Massachusetts militia during the Revolutionary War, although Festus was only fifteen at the time and had to falsify his age to be accepted. He served in the artillery, while Caesar may have been with Ethan Allen and the Green Mountain Boys. They had been neighbors of the Allens in Guilford. Festus, Sheldon says, "was inclined to festivity" and enjoyed fiddling which may have provided the trustees another excuse, besides race, to refuse him admission to the college. After the war, he settled on one of the Sunderland lots and married a white woman. It took Caesar may years to finally receive his government pension of $2.66 a month for his wartime service.

After most of the children had left home and the family was still in residence at Guilford in 1785, their white neighbors, the Noyce family, attempted to take over their property by intimidation, destroying fences and "burning haystacks." Lucy appealed directly to Governor Thomas Chittenden and his council, complaining of being "oppressed and injured by John and Ormas Noyce." It was decided by the council that the governor should write "to the Selectmen of the Town of Guilford recommending to them to take some effectual measures to protect the said Abijah, Lucy and family . . . "

The family then lived in relative peace until Abijah's death on the Guilford farm in 1794 at age 88. He did not live to hear Lucy's defense in court of his Sunderland grant, a court case which may well have made her famous in her lifetime. The accounts of the trial were passed along by spectators and by family members and became history which is "the myth agreed upon." There are no existing court records of *Eli Bronson vs Lucy Terry Prince.* However, the outcome of the trial is clear because the Sunderland property remained in the Prince family and was never challenged again.

The case was confusing because Vermont had problems in confirming state boundaries, especially with New Hampshire. The circuit courts in both states were plagued with fraudulent claims to land. Bronson's case against Lucy was based upon the validity of a Vermont land title.

Colonel Eli Bronson (Brownson), a neighbor of the Princes, claimed acreage that was a part of their Sunderland farm. The case was brought to the Circuit Court, Windsor, Vermont in 1797 or 1798. Lucy, now a widow of 67, was probably discouraged by family and friends from traveling to Windsor and making an issue of the case. It was assumed she would lose because of race and sex.

In the fictionalized biography of Lucy Terry Prince, *Black Woman* by Bernard and Jonathan Katz, they tell several stories about the trial that could be true because of the well-known personality of Associate Justice of the Supreme Court Samuel Chase. He was the former Chief Justice of the General Court of Maryland and narrowly missed being impeached by the State Assembly for frequently bullying people from the bench. As Justice of the U.S. Supreme Court, and an ardent Federalist, he would have articles of impeachment brought against him in the U.S. House of Representatives in 1804, encouraged by his political enemy, President Thomas Jefferson. The Senate trial subsequently failed to remove him from office, and he continued his bullying ways. His personality undoubtedly dominated Lucy's trial.

The political figures added another dimension to the trial. Lucy's lawyer, Isaac Tichenor would later become Governor of Vermont. Bronson had two attorneys: Stephen Bradley, who had been a U.S. Senator and Royall Tyler, a well-known Federalist like Chase, would also become Governor of Vermont.

Lucy had a copy of the original grant made to Abijah Prince However, Lucy's copy had not been authenticated with a seal of the county clerk in Portsmouth, New Hampshire, and was therefore invalid as evidence. The attorneys for Bronson objected to the evidence on the technicality of no seal on the document. In *Black Woman*, the Katz brothers write that Judge Chase asked his court clerk for his seal which he immediately affixed to the document, and entered into evidence. Of course, lawyers Bradley and Tyler would have objected strenuously . . . for a short period of time. Chase was known to have a short fuse when sitting on the bench, especially in dealing with trivialities and political opponents.

Bronson claimed that Bijah's 300 acres had been purchased for two pounds, three shillings at a tax sale by John Searles. John sold the property several days later to his brother Isaac. Lucy argued this sale was illegal because taxes had been paid and there was never public notice given of such a sale. It looked like a conspiracy to gain Sunderland property by these two men who bought the property. The illegality of the sale would invalidate Bronson's claim. The character of John Searles also was questioned because of a confession of counterfeiting quoted in *Black Woman.*

Lucy had Tichenor as her attorney, but she was permitted to argue her case before the jury. This was unheard of in Colonial America—a woman and a former slave appearing before a U. S. Justice of the Supreme Court pleading her case. Bronson's attorneys probably objected strenuously, but Justice Chase undoubtedly enjoyed the whole proceedings. When the jury found the complaint of Bronson to be "non-just," it also awarded Lucy court costs.

The case left such an impression that those in the courtroom never forgot the elderly, black woman who argued her own case and they passed the story along to their children.

Lucy moved to Sunderland in her seventies after losing the Guilford property to her neighbors when she could no longer pay the taxes on it. However, each spring, she would follow her heart and ride her horse over the Green Mountains to place flowers on Abijah's grave. She died in Sunderland at age 91 in 1821, before she could make her spring pilgrimage to Guilford, and before the lilacs bloomed.

Selected Bibliography

Hine, Darlene Clark, editor. *Black Women in America: An Historical Encyclopedia.* Volume II. Brooklyn, NY: Carlson Publishing Co., 1993.

Logan, Rayford W. and Michael R. Winston. *Dictionary of American Negro Biography.* New York: W. W. Norton and Co., 1982.

Holland, Josiah Gilbert. *Black Woman: A Fictionalized Biography of Lucy Terry Prince.* New York: Pantheon Books, 1973.

———. *A History of Western Massachusetts.* 2 volumes. Springfield: Samuel Bowles and Company, 1855. He mentions the court case and Chase's favorable comments to Lucy on her arguments to the jury.

Kaplan, Sidney. "Lucy Terry Prince." *The Black Presence in the Era of the American Revolution 1770-1800, National Portrait Gallery.* New York: Graphic Society, 1973.

Massachusetts Soldiers and Sailors in the Revolutionary War. Volume 12. Boston, MA: Writht and Potter Printing Company, 1904. Contains the military records of Caesar and Festus Prince.

Sheldon, George. "Negro Slavery in Old Deerfield." *New England Magazine*, (March 1893), pp. 55-57. The best reference on Lucy Terry Prince.

———. *A History of Deerfield.* Deerfield, Vt: 1896. Contains background of the town and Lucy's world. Abijah served in the Deerfield militia 1744-1748.

Walton, E. P. *Records of the Governor and Council State of the State of Vermont: Edited and published by authority of the state.* Volume III. Montpelier, VT: Steam Press of J. and J. M. Poland, 1875.

The Federal Cases in the Circuit and District Courts of the United States. St. Paul, MN: West Publishing Company, 1894. Book I lists Judge Samuel Chase "all circuit" from 1796 to 1801. Lucy's case, tried before Judge Chase, probably occurred within this five year period.

Blanford, Linda A. and Patricia Russell Evans, editors. *Supreme Court of the United States 1789-1980: An Index to Opinions Arranged by Justices.* Volume I, 1789-1902. Millwood, NY: Kraus International Publications, 1983.

Part III

MARY EDWARDS WALKER

"To live life to the end is not an easy task."
    Boris Pasternak

Women Short-Changed by History

Photograph of Mary Edwards Walker taken after the Civil War wearing the Medal of Honor. *Courtesy of the Hall of Heroes*, The Pentagon, Washington, D. C. Photograph by James Cole.

Mary Edwards Walker

Down a long corridor, into one of the "rings" in the heart of the Pentagon is the Hall of Heroes. The Hall is not mentioned in the welcome booklet issued by the Office of the Pentagon Building Manager nor in the information booklet, **The Pentagon**. But, here on marble walls of the halls are the names of those who have won the nation's highest military honor: The Congressional Medal of Honor. Men are so honored from every war, beginning with the Civil War, and ONE woman, the first and only woman to be awarded the Congressional Medal of Honor, Mary Edwards Walker.

In biographical dictionaries she is usually listed as "an eccentric," an advocate of bloomers, a feminist, a women's rights activist, and several additional unflattering descriptions. In reality she was intensely patriotic, committed to her profession of medicine, compassionate, determined, with an independent spirit envied by later generations of women. Because of these attributes and with the support of generals in the field who saw her at work in field hospitals, she was recommended for The Medal of Honor.

President Andrew Johnson awarded her the Medal on November 11, 1865. A board of retired generals reviewed her award in 1917 and, based on "revised standards," denied her the Medal and demanded that she return it. She refused and wore it every day of her life.

Finally, on June 10, 1977, 58 years after her death, the Medal was restored to her family by Army Secretary Clifford L. Alexander, Jr., and her name was inscribed on the Wall of Honor.

Women Short-Changed by History

MEDAL OF HONOR

UNITED STATES ARMY

The **Medal of Honor**, *Courtesy of Hall of Heroes*, The Pentagon, Washington, D. C. Photography by James Cole.

Mary Edwards Walker

Clutching the Medal of Honor, the elderly woman hurried down the Capital steps in Washington, D.C.. Oblivious to the stares at her outfit of black trousers, frock coat, and top hat, Mary Edwards Walker slipped and fell on the steps, cracking a hip bone. At age 84, the injury was serious and she never recovered from the accident. When she died two years later in February, 1919, she was still holding the Congressional Medal in spite of five retired generals on an army review board who had tried to take it from her.

She had been commended for her service as a contract field surgeon during the Civil War by Major Generals Sherman and Thomas, and at one time President Lincoln may have suggested some award. But, it was President Andrew Johnson who ordered "an honorable recognition of her services and sufferings" signed November 11, 1865.

The Congressional Record of February 9, 1880, hints at further assistance to the Union forces: "in accordance with a preconcerted arrangement entered into between her and the Federal officers, the petitioner thinking that she might obtain information while in the hands of the enemy which would be of value to the Federal officers."

She was taken prisoner while she moved back and forth between Union and Confederate lines, aiding civilians in Confederate-dominated countryside in addition to her assignments by the army while they were still in winter quarters in Tennessee.

After her capture, ranting at her, CSA Brigadier General William M.

Women Short-Changed by History

Gardner couldn't comprehend that the Union forces would contract "a female doctor with tongue enough for a regiment." He lectured her "until she cried" then had her sent to Castle Thunder prison, a converted tobacco warehouse in Richmond, Virginia. She later boasted of being exchanged after four months for a six-foot tall major while she barely topped five feet. Her months in prison, however, did leave scars; she suffered loss of vision and a dramatic weight decline.

Other women doctors and nurses contributed to the Union cause during the Civil War, but Dr. Mary was the only one to go directly to the battlefield as an "acting surgeon." Of singular purpose, she was bound to clash with others who were as determined as she to contribute their services. It would have been interesting to hear what Dr. Mary and Dorothea Dix discussed when their paths crossed. Miss Dix had been appointed Superintendent of Nurses in 1865. She immediately set down in a bulletin what would be expected of her charges: "No woman under thirty need apply to serve in government hospitals. All are required to be plain looking women . . . "

This certainly wasn't applicable to Mary Edwards Walker who was under thirty and described by contemporaries as "beautiful," "small," "well-rounded" with "sparkling eyes," "a fine complexion," and a "profusion of dark curls" which she decided to cut off when she entered service.

She chose to ignore the feud between Miss Dix and the Army's Medical Department when Miss Dix was given the authority to approve all nurses before they could serve, cutting down on the availability of medical help when it was needed most in the field. She also disagreed with other surgeons' handling of amputation procedures and the speed of such procedures. When overcome by the numbers of casualties in a battle, doctors believed themselves to be forced to chop off limbs and go on to the next patient. She encouraged soldiers to demand that a limb be saved, despite efforts of doctors to get on with the job. Most doctors with whom she worked every day (with very few exceptions) were determined to get rid of her.

Her appearance, her attitude and, above all, the fact that she was a woman doctor in a front-line hospital, kept her from obtaining a contract with the government which would have secured a salary and an acknowledgement of her abilities. So, much of her work was as an unpaid volunteer doctor.

When A. J. Rosa of the 52 Ohio Volunteers suddenly died, General Thomas appointed her as his successor. She was to report to Colonel Dan McCook at Gordon Mills, near Chattanooga. In January, 1864, before she left for the new assignment, the Medical Department of the Army ordered an examining board to review her education and experience. It planned to be unobjective and confrontational.

Doctors on the board called her "a medical monstrosity," and worse, "an encroachment on Victorian manhood."

Still, General Thomas and Assistant Surgeon General Wood supported her and protected her. Without a contract, but with her appointment, she went to winter quarters near Chattanooga where she was later captured by the Confederate forces.

What had brought this petite, determined young woman to study medicine, to go to Washington, to enlist in the Union army, and to give her life to causes which would not become fashionable until late in the 20th century.

She came from Puritan stock who claimed to have come over on the Mayflower. Alvah and Vesta Walker, her parents, believed in education and both had taught school, even beginning a free school when none was available for their five children.

As a child with nervous energy and a quick mind, she was her father's favorite. He took her on trips to town, encouraged her to read his books, including the medical manuals, and told her to set down her experiences and thoughts. To become a doctor was her goal from childhood, although she was discouraged by everyone except her parents. Her father disapproved of binding clothes, including the devil's handiwork, corsets. This may account for Mary's early design of her future dress code: a pair of loose trousers under a coat-dress which buttoned down the front and reached to just below the knees. This was not only her wedding outfit, but also her civilian clothing for the rest of her life.

In the army, she wore the officer's great coat, a Union blue uniform, pants with a gold stripe down the side, a felt hat with a cord of gold and the green surgeon's sash. Although, in later years, she was arrested several times for wearing men's clothing, as she continued to wear trousers. She maintained that she never tried to disguise herself as a man and that she would wear what she pleased.

An excerpt from 1866 in the *Home Journal* which later became *Town and Country Magazine*, concerning an arrest of Dr. Mary, was reprinted in its 150th birthday edition in 1996. It reported her appearance before the police commissioners against the officer who had arrested her. The article describes "an attractive woman" dressed in a broadcloth coat, but "from the waist downward, the cut of both coat and pantaloons is masculine. Her hat was "the merest chip of straw . . . her dainty parasol . . . everything but ample pantaloons, and coat, terminating at the knees, betokened the moderately fashionable woman."

She explained to the court that she wore her dress "from high moral principle." Of course, she was released and the officer was told, "Never arrest her again."

At President Chester A. Arthur's New Year's Day Reception in 1882, Mary arrived in a black broadcloth frock coat, trousers, tall silk hat and carrying a cane. In a picture of her taken in 1912 with a new version of the Congressional Medal of Honor around her neck, she is wearing a similar outfit - black tie, white shirt, black shoes, holding the "stove-pipe" hat—with her head held high, looking jaunty and satisfied with life. She was buried in this suit.

Her father was the one person who did not discourage her from going on to medical school after she had completed courses at Falley Seminary in New York. She had alternated her classes at Falley with teaching in the local school, saving her money for the next term. Males in her anatomy class would leave the classroom when she entered, but she took advantage of their absence by asking more questions. In 1853 at age 21, she was admitted to Syracuse Medical College, graduating two years later, the only woman in her class.

Then she fell in love with an older medical student who graduated with her and who was already established in Rome, N. Y. Dr. Arthur Miller did not mind that she took the word "obey" out of their marriage vows, nor the hyphenated name change, Dr. Walker-Miller (unheard of in 1854). He did not object to the untraditional wedding attire, trousers under a coat-dress. He had courted her in medical school and knew her preference in clothes. Although she was not a traditional homemaker because of her medical practice, she supervised the housekeeper and ran the household while she took care of her medical practice.

However, soon rumors of infidelities surfaced, which Dr. Miller quickly confirmed. Evidently, he was a ladies' man, but was still taken with his wife, so he encouraged her to join his lifestyle. Mary was humiliated. She left him and returned home to Oswego, N.Y. She began divorce proceedings in 1861, but the divorce was not final until 1869 because divorce was difficult and her civil war activities kept her on the move. Dr. Miller offered her financial help and attempted a reconciliation, but she rejected all his offers. Once was enough. She never fully trusted men again and scorned them for saying that they were "the natural protectors of women." She became increasingly active in issues affecting women.

She opposed the double standard (naturally), worked towards dress reform and women's rights, and advocated a national women's college. Obtaining more education was always a problem for her because colleges and universities were usually closed to women. Throughout her life, Dr. Mary in times of stress would turn to study. After leaving Miller, she moved in with friends in Iowa to attend Bowen Institute. She enrolled in a rhetoric class but was informed it was for men only. She joined a debating society and was prevented from debating. Suspended from the Institute, she returned to Rome, N.Y. and a limited practice.

Women Short-Changed by History

After the first battle of Bull Run, Mary closed her practice in Rome and went to Washington, D.C. where doctors were desperately needed. Surgeon General Clement A. Finley refused to consider her request for a commission, so she went from hospital to hospital seeking a position. On the second floor of the unfinished U.S. Patent Office she found a hospital for wounded Indiana and Vermont soldiers with Dr. J. N. Green in charge. With more than 100 men to care for and at the point of exhaustion, he was ready for help, paid or volunteered. He offered to give Mary part of his salary if she would stay. She refused his offer of money, continuing to work uncommissioned and without salary for several weeks.

She saw opportunities to help which were overlooked by her male counterparts, organizing a relief association for women who had no place to stay while visiting sons or husbands. She acquired supplies for her hospital including hundreds of checker boards which she made available to other hospitals.

Before moving on the Virginia headquarters of Major General Ambrose Burnside, where she was given a job as field surgeon, Mary took a refresher course and obtained a second medical degree at Hygeia Therapeutic College.

For the next two years she served near the front lines with the Union Army. She was at Fredericksburg, sometimes referred to as the worst fought battle of the Civil War. Six rail cars of wounded men in her care were transported from the front to Washington, D.C. after she ordered the engineer to move the train out. Without drugs, blankets, towels and with little water, she moved among the men trying to relieve suffering along the way. Upon arrival in Washington, she immediately wrote to their parents.

Still, no commission was offered to her in the United States Army.

In December, 1862, she was in Chattanooga working in the field hospital after the battle of Chicamauga. Once again, she requested a commission as an army doctor, but the army medical board maintained that she was "utterly unqualified for the position of medical officer." She later denied that there had ever been a hearing as to her qualifications.

Nevertheless, Major General George A. Thomas ignored the board's findings and appointed her to replace the assistant surgeon of the 52nd Ohio infantry after the death of the previous officer. His comment was "the young lady is very pretty and is said to thoroughly understand her profession."

On April 10, 1864, after serving for several months with the 52nd, she was taken prisoner by a young Confederate soldier while riding in the countryside. She maintained that she had been helping civilians in need, even though they were Confederate sympathizers. Or, as the Congressional Record hints, she may have been spying. Later, writing and speaking about the event, she elaborated on her adventures and it is not easy to discern fact from fiction. Did she perform "secret services" or obtain information that helped Major General William T. Sherman's forces from a "serious reversal?" There is no official record of her actions.

She was sent to Richmond, Va, nearly 700 miles from Ohio and imprisoned in Castle Thunder. The jailers didn't know what to do with the female prisoner who complained constantly about the poor diet of prisoners, especially the lack of fresh vegetables which may have caused her severe vision loss. Cornbread was "tiresome;" why not wheat bread and some cabbage for the prisoners? Her authoritative grumbling produced some results.

Four months later she was placed on a steamer, sent down the James River to Hampton Roads and exchanged for a major in the Confederate Army. This was to her an acknowledgement of her worth and her position as a contract surgeon. On the recommendation of General Thomas, the War Department paid her $432.38 for her services from March 11 to August 23 while she was a prisoner of war. In October, she was finally given a contract by the government as Acting Assistant Surgeon, U.S. Army, for $100 a month until the end of the war. But, she was not to return to the front.

After saying goodbye to her regiment, she was ordered to Louisville where she was put in charge of the Women's Prison Hospital. She hated it. From Louisville she was sent to Nashville to run an orphan asylum and aid refugee families, but this was not where she wanted to be. Finally, in March, 1865, a month before the end of the war, she was ordered to Gordon's Mill, Georgia. There General Dan McCook, who had been a colonel of the 52nd Ohio when she was stationed near Chattanooga, greeted her warmly. When he was absent for the troop review, he insisted she conduct the review—unheard of, but never forgotten by the troops.

Two months after Appomattox, Dr. Mary's contract with the army was cancelled at her request. The war was over and as many veterans discovered, they were not prepared for the transition to peacetime activities. Mary was no exception, although she was better prepared than most soldiers. She had been fighting for too many years for a place in a society that did not want to acknowledge a woman doctor, and a battlefield woman doctor at that. Paid in full, released from service, she wanted the promotion that others received with the severance paid. She had been exchanged in war for a major and she asked Secretary of War Stanton to grant her this promotion. However, as the judge advocate general ruled, she had never been an officer, so she couldn't be given any rank. Mary wrote to President Andrew Johnson just as she had written to President Lincoln asking for a commission, only to be turned down. She wrote more angry letters. The President asked Stanton if there were not some way to recognize her service. President Johnson ordered that a Medal of Honor be prepared for her.

On November 22, 1865, she received from President Andrew Johnson the Medal of Honor for meritorious service and the following citation:

> "***Whereas*, It appears from official reports that Dr. Mary E. Walker, a graduate of medicine, has rendered valuable service to the Government, and her efforts have been earnest and untiring in a variety of ways, and that she was assigned to duty**

and served as an Assistant-Surgeon, in charge of female prisoners at Louisville, Ky., upon the recommendation of Major Generals Sherman and Thomas, and faithfully served as Contract-Surgeon in the service of the United States, and has devoted herself with much patriotic zeal to the sick and wounded soldiers, both in the field and hospitals, to the detriment of her own health, and has also endured hardships as a prisoner of war four months in a Southern prison while acting as a Contract-Surgeon; and "*Whereas*, By reason of her not being a commissioned officer in the military service, a brevet or honorary rank can not, under existing laws, be conferred upon her; and

"*Whereas*, In the opinion of the President an honourable recognition of her services and sufferings should be made,

"IT IS ORDERED, That a testimonial thereof shall be hereby made, and given to the said Doctor Mary E. Walker, and that the usual medal of honour for meritorious services be given her.

"Given under my hand, in the city of Washington, D.C., this eleventh day of November, A.D. 1865.

Andrew Johnson, President
   By the President
   Edwin M. Stanton, Secretary of War

She wore that medal every day of her life.

Women Short-Changed by History

The Mary Edwards Walker display at the Hall of Heroes. *Courtesy of the Hall of Heroes*. The Pentagon, Washington, D. C. Photography by James Cole.

Perhaps this is where her biography should end. Mary Edwards Walker had been given the highest award her country could bestow; she was an attractive woman in her thirties; she was trained in a profession that offered a good income. But, she was restless and could not settle down. Her health was not good. Her former husband, Dr. Miller, now planned to divorce her, after she was the one who had tried to divorce him for years. She didn't know what she wanted to do with her life.

When she was invited to attend the annual meeting of the Society for the Promotion of Social Sciences in Manchester, England, she sailed with a friend, Susannah Way Dobbs, and Susannah's husband. In England and in Scotland, she visited operating rooms in the middle of surgeries to the astonishment of the staff. At the social science meeting, she talked on suffrage, dress reform and capital punishment. Although she was not a great public speaker, her presentations seemed to improve as she continued speaking. Press coverage was good; she made friends in Manchester; she was treated with respect by leading medical men in London.

After her friends returned to the United States, she continued lecturing and was even presented to Queen Victoria. And, yes, at her presentation she wore her "reform dress" of black silk, trimmed in velvet. She went on to Paris to visit hospitals. In that city she was accepted by the French as a medical humanitarian and a heroine.

It was only when she returned home to the United States that everything went wrong for her. She had been treated with respect and even enthusiasm in London, Paris and Glasgow. Back home, she was faced with a counter-divorce suit which was won by her former husband. She felt humiliated again, especially after all of her efforts to divorce him.

Her medical practice had failed. She went on the lecture circuit, but few people would pay to hear of her Civil War adventures. They wanted to forget this war with more than one million soldiers dead and maimed. In Kansas City, Mo. and in New Orleans she was arrested for wearing trousers, although both cases were later dismissed. The lecture tour ended in Texas with Mary broke and without speaking engagements.

She went back to Washington, D.C. where she studied law and lobbied for women's rights. Living there, she shared a house with Mrs. Belva Lockwood, a prominent suffragette. Tax reform for self-supporting women earning less than $500 a year became an issue for her.

Her energies were directed to make Congress aware of the women who had served in the Civil War and who were now ignored or forgotten completely. Why shouldn't they receive pensions and land given to men? Why shouldn't they have the right to vote? What had been one of her many interests before the war now became a driving force. Her other causes were not forgotten and she fought for them all, wearing men's clothing long after other women had put away their "bloomers." She became "a bothersome eccentric," roaming the halls of Congress, button-holing legislators who were determined to get on with business and industry in the Gilded Age.

The army awarded her $8.50 a month because of her damaged eyes, but that was the total amount of the pension she received. Nurses who had served in the war were granted $12 and Mary, as a physician, was asking for $20. From 1872 and for the rest of her life, Mary sought compensation for the money she should have received for her expenses as a volunteer surgeon and "for money expended in behalf of the sick and wounded." The bills either died in Congressional committees or passed one house before dying in the other legislative body.

Eight years after the first bill for her relief was introduced, it was suggested that a bill just might pass if she dressed like other women. Of course, she refused the proposal. Not until 1898 did she finally receive a $20 a month pension.

Lack of funds did not alter the direction of her life.

She took on the tobacco lobby, and in 1881 ran for the U.S. Senate listing her qualifications as a "brain not numbed by drugs, liquor or tobacco." She lost, but added another cause to her agenda—direct election of Senators.

She marched with the suffragettes to get the right to vote and shared platforms at conventions with Lucy Stone and Susan B. Anthony. When marching and petitions didn't bring about the vote, Mary broke with the leadership of the National Suffrage Association. This may be the reason that her name is seldom seen in the ranks of the association and why she was never given credit for her efforts. She consistently maintained that the right of women to vote was in the Constitution and no amendment was needed. In a monograph, "Crowning Constitutional Argument," she wrote that in the section of the Declaratory Act, the clause prohibiting any state from making laws in conflict with existing provisions included the franchise. She believed that Senator Charles Sumner and Chief Justice Salmon P. Chase agreed with her argument. She broke off her friendship with Belva Lockwood over this issue and became a solitary figure in the halls of power in men's clothing demanding equal rights for women.

| 46TH CONGRESS, | SENATE. | REPORT |
| 2d Session. | | No. 237. |

IN THE SENATE OF THE UNITED STATES.

FEBRUARY 9, 1880.—Ordered to be printed.

Mr. FARLEY, from the Committee on Pensions, submitted the following

REPORT:

The Committee on Pensions, to whom was referred the petition of Dr. Mary E. Walker, for increase of pension, beg leave to make the following report:

The petitioner was assigned to duty as hospital nurse, March 12, 1864, after an examination by a board of medical officers convened at Chattanooga, who reported that she was not competent to perform the duties of an assistant surgeon, her knowledge of medicine and surgery being very little, if any, more than that of the ordinary housewife.

It appears that while acting in this capacity she wandered outside of the lines, and was taken prisoner, in accordance with a preconcerted arrangement entered into between her and the Federal officers, the petitioner thinking that she might obtain information while in the hands of the enemy which would be of value to the Federal officers.

She returned in about four months, and, on recommendation of General George H. Thomas, the War Department allowed her $80 per month from March 11, 1864, to August 24, 1864. She then returned to Louisville, and was employed a few months in the female prisoners' hospital, receiving $100 per month for her services. The petitioner claimed to suffer from weakness of the eyes, produced by insufficient food and exposure while a prisoner, and upon the report of a board of examining surgeons of the Pension Bureau, she was allowed, and now receives, $8.50 per month, that amount being one-half pension for a contract surgeon. She was regarded as constructively in the service as a contract-surgeon, by virtue of the recommendation of General Thomas above referred to, which recommendation was acted on by the War Department. There was some doubt expressed in the medical evidence as to whether the weakness of the eyes was occasioned by exposure in the service, from age, or other causes.

No evidence is offered in addition to that which went before the Pension Bureau. From all the facts in the case, your committee recommend that the prayer of petitioner be not granted.

Denial of additional pension for Mary Edwards Walker. *United States Senate, 46th Congress, February 9, 1880.*

In politics, she was independent and outspoken, but usually voted Democratic. She admired President Lincoln and campaigned for him in the election of 1864 despite the fact that he had denied her appeal for a commission in the army. She considered him a man of principle but could not say the same for Ulysses S. Grant. President Grant died of throat cancer, probably from prolonged smoking of cigars, which Mary maintained were "pure poison."

She had lived in Washington, D.C. long enough to form definite opinions on the profession of government service. She knew that "many of the Congressmen were in their dotage and President Theodore Roosevelt was unworthy of passing notice." She liked politics and after her candidacy for the Senate, she ran for the House of Representatives and lost.

When Chester A. Arthur became President following the assassination of McKinley, she was given a government appointment to the mail room of the pension's office in the Department of the Interior. She lasted ten months as a clerk. She complained of the inefficiency and lack of ventilation in the workplace. Her eyes hurt. Returning from sick leave, she was locked out of her office. Dr. Mary appealed directly to Arthur, but he refused to see her. Only years later was she given credit for her idea of a post card receipt for registered letters. Her suggestion for return addresses on packages was adopted by the post office and is mandatory today.

With her limited funds and no longer able to see well, Mary almost became part of the Vaudeville circuit. She did give speeches on women's rights and the advantages of wearing men's clothing. Wherever she spoke, she always wore her Congressional Medal of Honor. This infuriated some critics who said, "There is something grotesque about her appearance on a stage built for freaks." She had written two books detailing her thoughts on everything from sex to the Apostle Paul's distorted view of women. But, no one was interested in her opinions or her books.

However, every lost cause forced her into action: She opposed the annexation of Hawaii and proposed Congressional representation for the District of Columbia. She infuriated her neighbors by circulating a petition seeking clemency for the anarchist who shot President McKinley.

When her brother died, she was left the management of the family farm. Her sister Aurora tried to help out with her finances. After Aurora's death, she must have felt really alone. ..older, stubborn, opinionated, hounded by the press . . . the worst was yet to come.

In 1917, at the request of Congress, the Board of Medal Award, a panel of retired generals, reviewed the Medal of Honor recipients and rescinded 917 Medals, including that of Dr. Mary. The standards for receiving the Medal had been revised to include only "actual combat with the enemy." In Mary's situation, this was vague because she had been taken as a prisoner of war. The board further stated that her "service does not appear to have been distinguished in action or otherwise." Too bad no one bothered to read the Congressional Record or the memorials passed by Congress or the hundreds of letters from servicemen. She was told that it was a crime to wear the Medal. This did not prevent her from wearing the Medal every day of her life. Her niece, Anne Walker, in an interview with the *Dallas Morning News*, said her aunt told the panel, "You may have it back over my dead body and then only if you can get it back from rigor mortis."

She appealed the board's decision to Congressmen and to the War Department. She continued to give speeches, wearing the Medal. She gave tours of her home in Oswego, but family squabbles, money problems, even accusations of insanity further isolated her. The cruelty of some Oswego residents was evident when she was refused membership in the local DAR. Undaunted, Mary went to St. Louis for acceptance into the organization there.

Unable to turn the family farm into a school or a tuberculosis sanitarium, refused by the New York State Historical Association as a trust home and without help in maintaining it, her home became rundown and her situation tragic.

```
                    DEPARTMENT OF THE INTERIOR
                         BUREAU OF PENSIONS
                                    WASHINGTON, D. C., January 2, 1915.
        SIR: Please answer, at your earliest convenience, the questions enumerated below. The information
    is requested for future use, and it may be of great value to your widow or children. Use the inclosed
    envelope, which requires no stamp.
                            Very respectfully,

                                              [signature]
                                                                Commissioner.
        MARY E. WALKER,
              OSWEGO    N Y
        142715
                        R R 7                          MAR 16 1915
```

No. 1. Date and place of birth? *Oswego N.Y.*
The name of organizations in which you served? *A. A. Surgeons Regular Army*
No. 2. What was your post office at enlistment? *Oswego N.Y.*
No. 3. State your wife's full name and her maiden name. *I am not a man*
No. 4. When, where, and by whom were you married? *I am not a man*
No. 5. Is there any official or church record of your marriage?
    If so, where? *I am not a man*
No. 6. Were you previously married? If so, state the name of your former wife, the date of the marriage, and the date and place of her death or divorce. If there was more than one previous marriage, let your answer include all former wives. *No I am not a man*

I am not a man

No. 7. If your present wife was married before her marriage to you, state the name of her former husband, the date of such marriage, and the date and place of his death or divorce, and state whether he ever rendered any military or naval service, and, if so, give name of the organization in which he served. If she was married more than once before her marriage to you, let your answer include all former husbands. *I am not a man*

No. 8. Are you now living with your wife, or has there been a separation? *I am not a man*
No. 9. State the names and dates of birth of all your children, living or dead. *I am not a man*

Pension Application of Mary Edwards Walker. Note her numerous protests of "I am not a man."

She survived until February 21, 1919. She was buried in the small cemetery outside Oswego wearing her formal attire of trousers and frock coat. Of the few present at the interment, not a single member of the armed forces was present, nor a representative of any suffrage group that she had fought for and supported.

The army owed her a full military funeral.

Members of her family and women in the publishing field who knew her history did not forget her. Several U.S. senators carried her fight for reinstatement of the Medal to the Defense Department. In the army's consideration of the restoration Medal of Honor to Dr. Mary Edwards Walker, a spokesperson was quoted as saying, "Dr Walker *probably* had been a victim of sex discrimination." (Italics are the author's.)

Finally, from the public affairs office of the Assistant Secretary of Defense, came the announcement of: Restoration of Award. On June 10, 1977 Army Secretary Clifford L. Alexander, Jr. approved the recommendation of the Army Board for Correction of Military Records of May 4, 1977, to restore the Medal of Honor to Dr. Mary E. Walker.

She would never have doubted her right to be on the Wall of Honor in the Hall of Heroes.

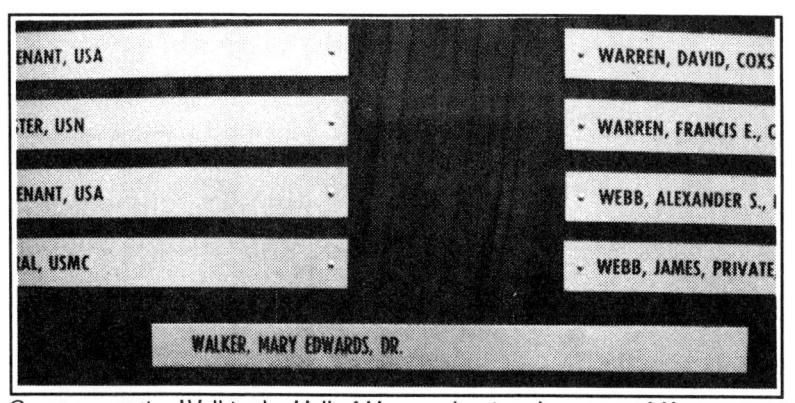

Commemorative Wall in the Hall of Heroes showing the name of Mary Edwards Walker, Dr. *Courtesy of the Hall of Heroes.* The Pentagon, Washington, D. C. Photography by James Cole.

Women Short-Changed by History

Entrance to the Hall of Heroes, The Pentagon, Washington, D. C. *Courtesy of the Hall of Heroes.* Photograph by James Cole.

Selected Bibliography

Sweeney, Julia. Interview with Anne Walker, great grand niece of Mary Edwards Walker. *Dallas Times Herald*. 30 June 1976. The first time I heard the name of Dr. Mary.

Snyder, Charles McCool. *Dr. Mary Walker: The Little Lady in Pants*. New York: Arno Press, 1974. Snyder interviewed people who remembered Dr. Mary.

Malone, Dumas, editor. *Dictionary of American Biography*, Vol. XIX. New York: Charles Scribners' Sons, 1936.

The National Encyclopedia of American Biography, Vol. XIII. New York: James T. White & Company, 1906.

James, Edward T., editor. *Notable American Women, 1607–1950.* Vol. III. Cambridge, MA: Belknap Press of Harvard University, 1971.

Leonard, Elizabeth D. *Yankee Women: Gender Battles in the Civil War.* New York: W. W. Norton, 1994.

Town and Country, 150th Anniversary Edition. Reprint from *Home Journal* (parent magazine), 1866. An account of Mary Edwards Walker's arrest and release for wearing the "reform dress."

Above and Beyond: A History of the Medal of Honor from the Civil War to Vietnam. Boston: Boston Publishing Co., 1985.

Poynter, Lida. "Dr. Mary Walker, M. D. Pioneer Woman Physician." *Medical Woman's Journal: A History of Women in Medicine,* Bertha Selmon, M. D., editor. October, 1946.

"Can a Woman Battle Doctor Regain a Male-Only Medal." *Washington Star,* 30 April 1976.

"Medal of Honor Restored to Civil War Woman Doctor." *The Washington Post.* 11 Jun 1977.

Welcome to the Pentagon: Department of Defense, 1943–1993. Washington, D. C.: Washington Headquarters Services, 1993.

United States National Archives, Washington, D.C. File #142715, Case 2656 of Mary E. Walker, Acting Assistant and Contract

Surgeon, U. S. Army official correspondence with War Department, 1876; Department of the Interior, 1912, 1915, 1919; Assistant Secretary of Defense, restoration of award, 1977.

United States Congress. Fifty-fifth Congress, Second Session. House of Representatives, Report No. 1400, Report to accompany HR 9732, 23 May 1898.

United States Congress. Forty-sixth Congress, Second Session. United States Senate. Report No. 237, 9 February 1880.

Walker Papers, Walker Collection, Syracuse University, Syracuse, New York. This collection contains documents pertaining to the life of Mary Edwards Walker and includes letters, pictures, diplomas, etc.

Lawson, Dorris Moore. "Mary E. Walker: A Biographical Sketch." Master of Arts in History thesis, unpublished manuscript, Syracuse University, June 1954.

Part IV

SARAH JOSEPHA HALE

"If we mean to have heroes, statesmen and philosophers, we should have learned women."
                    Abigail Adams

Women Short-Changed by History

Sarah Josepha Hale

Sarah Josepha Hale was a lady. She wore dove-grey silk gowns and side curls. She lived by the Victorian conventions of her day. She enjoyed "polite society" and her reputation was spotless. As one of the first women editors in the United States, she wrote in the February, 1832, **Ladies' Magazine**: "I consider every attempt to induce women to think they have a just right to participate in the public duties of government as injurious to their best interests and derogatory to their character . . . " She did not change her mind of this subject.

In contrast to her views on women's suffrage, her ideas on education are today accepted practices in public education. She taught boys and girls together. She conducted a day care center for children of working mothers. She encouraged women to be teachers at a time when only men were thought to be capable instructors of the young. She joined the movement to win property rights for married women.

She edited the first nationally successful women's magazine with departments for poetry, home decorating, editorials and, of course, her column, signed by The Lady Editor.

To think that she might be remembered, if at all, only as the author of the children's ditty, "Mary Had a Little Lamb" is an injustice.

More important than Mary and her lamb, Sarah Josepha Buell Hale gave us Thanksgiving Day as we have celebrated it since 1863.

Women Short-Changed by History

Sarah Josepha Hale

    Poverty and home-schooling were the two major elements of her childhood. Her mother insisted that Sarah Buell read the Bible, Shakespeare, Bunyan and Milton. Her older brother, Horatio, brought home books from Dartmouth College and helped her expand her knowledge of the world beyond the small New Hampshire village of Newport. Her father, a Revolutionary War veteran in poor health, gave up farming to open a tavern. He eventually failed at this, too.

    To help put food on the table, Sarah started a small school for children in the community, teaching boys and girls together. This was unheard of in 1806. Men taught boys, and girls stayed home to cook and to sew. Sarah believed in education for girls and young women that would expand their opportunities beyond making hats and "dressing gentle folks." Why not give them the same schooling as boys, so that they could read and write. Her curriculum also included exercise, hiking and picnics.

    Sarah may have written Mary's Lamb at this time to encourage children to get to school on time. The ditty was later printed in one of her books, *Poems for Our Children* and signed SJH.

    Her mother and sister died of tuberculosis on the same day in 1811. Her oldest brother, Charles, was lost at sea. Her father's health, as well as the tavern business, was failing. At twenty-five, an impoverished school teacher, was rescued from spinsterhood by a handsome young lawyer, David Hale. He lived in a nearby town and sometimes stayed at the tavern before its demise, probably to be near Sarah.

Descriptions of Sarah at twenty-five and through the years is invariably the same: short, slender, vital, with an oval face, beautiful eyes, long brown hair that never turned grey. Her grandson said she carried herself "like a duchess of fiction." She did not consider matrimony while providing for the members of the family, always her first concern. Without them, she turned to David Hale who wanted to care for her. They married in 1813.

By all accounts this was a very good marriage. They had five children within nine years. They studied French, botany and geology together in the evening and with friends began a small literary society. They hiked the New England countryside together and discussed events of the day and her poetry which David encouraged her to write.

Plagued with respiratory problems, David developed pneumonia a few weeks preceding the birth of their fifth child, William George Hale. He died unexpectedly. Suddenly, Sarah was left alone, with five children to raise, no money, and wonderful memories of the life they had shared.

Sarah Buell Hale put aside grief and began again. She had five children to support and educate. Masonic friends of David's helped Sarah and her sister-in-law, Hannah, set up a "ladies millinery." But more important, members of the literary society paid for publishing her first book of poetry, *The Genius of Oblivion and Other Original Poems,* under the name Cornelia. This brought recognition and modest success. Enough that she could cease making ladies' hats and write the novel *Northwood* in 1827, revised in 1852.

Although out of date and out of print, *Northwood* is of interest to historians, because it points out the economic rivalries and cultural differences between North and South three decades before the Civil War. More accurately she thought the book might be "a reference describing faithfully the age" in which she lived. In it, Sarah devoted an entire chapter to a Thanksgiving Day, especially the dinner which she described in detail as to the setting of the table and the preparation of the food.

Chapter eight of *Northwood* begins with a quote from William Goldsmith: "Thine, Freedom, thine, the blessings pictured here." This was why Sarah believed in a national day of Thanksgiving, celebrating her county and giving thanks for the blessings bestowed upon it.

Many families today plan their meal, as Sarah planned hers, perhaps not so elaborately: with a table covered by a white damask cloth and "provisions sufficient for a multitude, because it was an honor for a man to sit down to his Thanksgiving dinner surrounded by a large family" "Roasted turkey took precedence, being placed at the head of the table. Bowls of gravy and plates of vegetables—a goose and a pair of ducklings, a huge chicken pie, plates of pickles, preserves and butter; plum pudding, custards and pies. Yet the pumpkin pie occupied the most distinguished niche." The final course included cake, sweet meats, fruits, currant wine, (in moderation, of course), cider and ginger beer.

After the blessing by the father, the eating "commenced in earnest."

"Thanksgiving, like the Fourth of July, should be considered a national festival and observed by all our people."

It is ironic that her concern for the Union was never reflected in articles and editorials she wrote for the *Ladies' Magazine* and for *Godey's*. Editorial policy prevented the mention of politics or of slavery. However, in two other books, she supported the American Colonization Society which raised money to send freedmen to Liberia in Africa. She thought that it was wrong "to appropriate other men's property" without compensation and to set slaves free "without education."

In *Northwood,* her hero, Sidney, returning to New England after living on a southern plantation says, "The black man could learn correct English . . . but meanwhile he vulgarizes the language of white children by teaching them his own idiomatic jargon." Sidney blamed white southern illiteracy as a consequence of slavery. So did Sarah, but she never publicly stated it. Instead, she wanted people to contribute to a special Thanksgiving church offering to finance colonization by freed

Christian American slaves.

Northwood was widely read and reprinted in London. The Reverend John Lewis Lake, after reading Sarah's book, thought her talent could be used in editing a women's magazine that he hoped to begin publishing in 1828. The job necessitated a move to Boston, which Sarah hesitated to do. After some consideration, it was a good move in terms of educating her children, and that was her first priority.

While editing and writing full time, she was successful in seeing that her children had the best education available. Her oldest son, David, graduated from West Point in 1833. He died suddenly in 1839. Her second son, Horatio, was named for her brother, the Dartmouth valedictorian. Horatio was a Harvard graduate, a philologist, an expert on several languages, and an explorer. The youngest son, William, who was born after his father's death, sat on the Texas Supreme Court. Her older daughter had a successful girls' school in Philadelphia, while the younger married a doctor. As her children were studying, Sarah advised Mathew Vassar on the founding of his women's college, insisting that he dispense with the word female from its name, which he did.

For thirteen years she marked "the progress of female improvement," and cherished "the effusions of female intellect" in the *Ladies' Magazine.* Later, it was called the *American Ladies' Magazine,* to differentiate it from the British counterpart. She composed much of the copy herself, because she refused to steal articles from other magazines, a common practice of the day. She encouraged young authors including a classmate of her son David. Edgar Allen Poe had submitted some early poems to Sarah and she told him that he had talent and to continue writing. After his death, she gave money to the mother of Poe's child-bride, Virginia. In 1845 Sarah aided in the passage of copyright laws that were to protect authors from plagerism.

Although Sarah praised "meekness" as a "women's highest ornament," she was not shy about raising money for the completion of the Bunker Hill monument and the founding of the Seaman's Aid Society of Boston, which fed and clothed widows of sailors and their children. Later she would be involved in saving Mount Vernon, George Washington's home. She loved the rummage sale, and introduced this means of making money to the ladies of New England.

Sarah believed man may be physically stronger and "coarsely sensual," but woman was superior in "sensibility, intuition, piety and virtue." Therefore, women should be educated to reach their "more excellent and spiritual empire." Education of children should naturally be the province of women. The *Ladies' Magazine* supported normal schools for women, the kindergarten movement and education for the deaf.

She was interested in and promoted labor-saving inventions for women like the sewing machine and the washing machine. She took advantage of technological advances in publishing and was the first editor to use colored fashion plates. From the French, she borrowed "lingerie" for ladies' unmentionables in the magazine.

In spite of her innovations, the *Ladies' Magazine* was not a financial success. However, they did impress a young Frenchman who wanted her to edit his new publication, *Godey's Lady's Book*. He even offered to buy out the *American Ladies' Magazine,* make her editor of *Godey's* and let her edit it in Boston. This was an offer she couldn't refuse. He combined the two periodicals in 1837. Four years later, she finally moved to Philadelphia after her youngest son graduated from Harvard. She remained *Godey's* editor for forty years.

Conservative, restrained in its editorials, *Godey's* would never print anything "to undermine the position of husbands." Sarah's home with husband, David, had been "the sacred residence designed by divine goodness." This home became the ideal she encouraged other to emulate through the magazine. Sarah wore black mourning for David the remainder of her life and never considered the possibility of remarriage.

Sarah's work with *Godey's* became her passion, especially centering on education for women. Writing from experience, she editorialized,

Women Short-Changed by History

"Every young woman in our land should be qualified by some accomplishment which she may teach or some art or profession she can follow, to support herself creditably, should the necessity occur."

And a woman needed to be in good health to support herself creditably. No more swooning genteelly, no more tight corsets, but sensible clothes, proper diet and exercise, yes, exercise and fresh air. In her columns she praised Elizabeth Blackwell, the first woman in the United States to earn a medical degree. Here was a woman who put into practice what Sarah had been preaching. But her Victorian upbringing permitted her only limited praise of the work of women doctors. Her reasoning was that male doctors should not treat female patients. Women needed their own physicians "to treat the more intimate female complaints."

As an editor, she was never too far ahead of her readers. She was never confrontational, always positive. Especially she avoided politics. As a businesswoman she was still the product of the cultural and social milieu of her era. And she was, above all, a lady. She did not approve of whiskers, and warned women against kissing a man with a mustache. Her formula for hand lotion, which she passed on to her readers, was lard, rosewater, and coconut milk. She recommended vinegar soaked in strips of brown paper to ward off wrinkles.

Sarah Hale had few critics. One of them, Elizabeth Oakes Smith, claimed her for her mentor. Elizabeth Smith was famous at the time for being the first woman to lecture before lyceums in the country. She had a wide following and conversed with poets and philosophers. She described Sarah's talents "of high order," but "without genius." She was "generous to young writers" but "they were apt to outgrow their kind mentor." Sarah, wrote Elizabeth, decreed a career that was "a tribute to the respectabilities, decorum and moralities of life devoid of its enthusiasms."

These words may have been prompted by Sarah's refusal to hear Elizabeth speak in Philadelphia because she thought that a woman speaking in public before an audience was "presumptuous" and "indecorous." Their friendship remained, but Elizabeth wrote that Sarah "was always pleasantly on the safe and accepted side."

Sarah invited her to write for the *Ladies' Magazine,* which Elizabeth sometimes did. Of her encouragement of young writers, she wrote that Sarah "notwithstanding her conventionalism, built better than she knew, in that she awakened the dormant energies of others." And "she was without pretension and without vanity."

As Sarah worked at editing and writing, there was no mention in *Godey's* of the Civil War dividing the country; no word on slavery or Lincoln's Emancipation Proclamation. But she never forgot the idea of a day of Thanksgiving for the nation. In an editorial in 1846, during President Polk's administration, she began urging her readers to write to the president, to governors and to other public officials to declare a Thanksgiving Day. Her exertions did not cease.

Five years later she could announce that twenty-nine states had observed a special day, but Sarah wanted a presidential proclamation. With the Civil War looming in 1858 her appeal asked "..would it not be a renewal pledge of love and loyalty to the Constitution of the United States which guaranties peace, prosperity and perpetuity to our great Republic." The next editorial in 1861 called for a day of peace, just one day to "lay aside our enmities and strifes."

It took two more years of bloodletting and the Battle of Gettysburg, which inspired Lincoln's Gettysburg Address, before Lincoln acted on Sarah's plea. President Abraham Lincoln proclaimed Thanksgiving Day on October 3, 1863. He gave Sarah credit for encouraging him to do so. Sarah was then seventy-five years old and still editing.

After the assassination for Lincoln, the Lady Editor went to see President Andrew Johnson, urging him to continue the celebration on the last Thursday in November. After Johnson, she saw President Ulysses S. Grant, just to remind him that he and the nation should remember to give thanks. He continued the Thanksgiving proclamations as did succeeding presidents.

Women Short-Changed by History

Today, Thanksgiving is celebrated on the fourth Thursday of November in the same way Sarah foresaw it in *Northwood*.

She remained editor of *Godey's* until it was sold in 1877. She had written cook books, short stories, verse anthologies, biographical sketches and had guided women's tastes in literature, home improvement, fashion, music, and decorating for half a century. Sarah retired in December of 1877 at the age of eighty-nine.

She wrote, "Having reached my ninetieth year, I bid farewell to my countrywomen, with the hope that this work of half a century may be blessed to the furtherance of their happiness and usefulness in their Divinely appointed spheres." Sarah died the following April.

Her country takes for granted a day designed by Sarah Josepha Hale, and never remembers that her persistence made Thanksgiving Day possible. For a lady of New Hampshire granite, mixed with compassion, dignity and intelligence, she would never have expected to the memorialized. But certainly a simple thank you would be considered proper.

Selected Bibliography

Hale, Sarah Josepha. *Northwood.* New York: Johnson Reprint Company, 1970. This was her first and only novel. It is a description of the world as seen by Sarah, and it contains the only comment, in print, that mentions slavery. First published in 1827 and again in 1852, Sarah describes in *Northwood* an idealized Thanksgiving, the day as we would like it to be.

National Society of the Colonial Dames of America in the State of Texas. Compiled by the Historical Activities Committee, Zelva Compton Laird, Chairman, prepared by Mrs. Gerald Notebroom. *Women Colonial and Pioneer.* Dallas, TX: Benj. Franklin Printing Services, 1982. The first time I read of Sarah Josepha Hale.

James, Edward T., editor. *Notable American Women, 1606-1950.* Vol. II. Cambridge, MA: The Belknap Press of Harvard University, 1971.

Ecker, Betty Cook. "Our Thanksgiving Debt to a Liberated Lady." *The Dallas Morning News*, 19 November 1972.

Tait, Elaine. "A Feminist Even the Men Will Honor." The Philadelphia Inquirer , 7 February 1973.

Finley, Ruth E. *The Lady of Godey's.* Philadelphia, PA: J. B. Lippincott Company, 1931.

Fryatt, Norma R. *Sarah Josepha Hale.* New York: Hawthorne Books, Inc., 1975.

Wyman, Mary Alice, editor. *Selections from the Autobiography of Elizabeth Oakes Smith.* Lewiston, ME: Lewiston Journal Company, 1924. Elizabeth Oakes Smith was a young contemporary of Sarah's who sometimes described her as a mentor and at other times hinted at her imperfections, especially that of being too set in her ways to speak out on social issues.

Women Short-Changed by History

Part V

VICTORIA CLAFLIN WOODHULL

"Veni, Vidi, Vici."
Gaius Julius Caesar

Women Short-Changed by History

Victoria Claflin Woodhull. Presumed from clothing description and age to have been taken at the time of her appearance before the United States Senate in 1871.

Victoria Claflin Woodhull

When Victoria Claflin Woodhull Blood Martin looked over her country estate at Bredon's Norton, she should have been satisfied with her life. She ruled one of the oldest and most beautiful estates in Southwestern England. She had entertained the Prince of Wales, later Edward VII, in the sixteenth century Mansion House where Sir Walter Scott had once lived. The Old Manor House on the estate may have dated back to the Norman Conquest. Victoria owned it all, and she had inherited from her third husband the estate and the wealth to maintain it. In her eighties, at last, she was admitted to "high society." She involved herself in Anglo-American relations, urging United States intervention in World War I. When she died at eighty-nine, sitting upright in her favorite chair, defying death, her will specified cremation and that her ashes be scattered in the Atlantic Ocean, midway between "my two countries."

Can this be the same woman who was called "Mrs. Satan," "the terrible siren," "the Queen of Prostitutes," "that sinful woman" in the United States where she was born and came to fame or infamy fifty years previously? How could she repudiate everything she had so righteously upheld and then deny vigorously and with lawsuits that she had ever said or done the things printed about her in newspapers or in magazines. Her adaptability was a marvel.

Suffragettes and feminists should have demanded her inclusion in history books: the first woman to run for the Presidency, the first *woman stockbroker, a lone woman standard-bearer for free love, the newspaper publisher who first ran the Communist Manifesto in the United States.*

Instead, Victoria Woodhull is not even a footnote in most history texts. For her, this would have been the ultimate tragedy.

Certainly her dysfunctional family influenced her life. Her childhood could not have been pleasant nor normal. Victoria said that she had visions from the age of three. This may have been a means of removing herself from the family. Angels, the devil, prophets came to her regularly, and they enabled her to escape temporarily from the strange household which alternated between praying and scheming. One mystic visitor in a Greek tunic promised her a mansion, wealth and leadership. Later, he would return to her and write his name, Demosthenes, on a table, leading her to New York, but that would be in the future. For the present in Homer, Ohio, the Claflin family was "different" enough to be ostracized. However, mother Roxy considered herself of the elect and saved; therefore, she and her children could do no wrong.

Sometime in the 1840s, the family's grist mill burnt to the ground after being insured beyond its worth. In Homer, people used the word arson, and father Buck Claflin quickly left town without his troublesome family when there were threats of "tar and feathers." In Emanie Sachs' book about Victoria, she wrote that some citizens of Homer gave the Claflins a benefit just "to get them out of town." And, from there they went roaming, never welcome anywhere for long.

Victoria's sister, Tennie, lived with relatives for a while until she began seeing the future or secrets others wanted hidden. Then father Buck appeared and charged money for her visions. The sisters later joined forces in Mt. Gilead, Ohio to lift tables and to encourage spirit visitation. For a time the family lived with sister Margaret Ann and her husband Enos Miles who came from a reputable family. What a brawling, tempestuous household that must have been. Enos divorced Margaret Ann when divorce was rare, probably to save his sanity. And, the family moved on.

At the age of fourteen, Victoria married Dr. Canning Woodhull. From all accounts, except Victoria's, he was a nice, gentle man. Twenty years later, when her biography was written by a love-smitten puritan Theodore Tilton, Dr. Woodhull had become an alcoholic monster. Alcoholic he was, but a monster, hardly. After the birth of a son, Byron, the Cannings moved to California. Victoria said that she worked to help support them as a seamstress, cigar girl, and actress (?). However, one evening she had a vision of sister Tennie calling her, and she answered the spirit voices by heading for home immediately.

In the several biographies of Victoria, the Civil War is not mentioned, and it is difficult to trace the family after Victoria's return with Canning and Byron to Cincinnati. Tennie had been indicted for manslaughter in Ottawa, Illinois because her "cancer cure" did not, so the clan changed strategies and location quickly. Victoria and Tennie advertised themselves as clairvoyants in Cincinnati, but were accused of prostitution and blackmail, so they reappeared in Chicago where they were evicted on "suspicious" activities. They traveled through Arkansas, Missouri, Kansas and Tennessee, constantly fighting, Buck gambling, and the sisters holding seances. Back in Chicago again, they were evicted for "fraudulent fortune-telling," although there were rumors of prostitution.

During these years, Byron accidently fell on his head from a second-story window and survived although he was brain-damaged from the fall. His father, despite his alcoholic haze, cared for him lovingly. Victoria also had a daughter by Canning, Zulu Maud, whom she called "the light of my life."

In 1865 or 1866 Victoria met Colonel James Harvey Blood at a seance in St. Louis, where he was the City Auditor. He was also a Civil War veteran, a Spiritualist and a believer in "free love." He was described by contemporaries as "gallant and courteous." Compared to the Claflin clan, this must have been a shock to Victoria. He was also married. After meeting Victoria, he abandoned wife, children and job and took off with Victoria in a covered wagon to travel the Ozarks, while Canning took care of Byron and Zulu Maud.

When the couple returned from this idyll, they divorced their spouses in 1868 and lived together an husband and wife for many years, but probably did not marry, except "by the powers of the air." Canning Woodhull moved out. This was a terrible time for Byron. He did not know his neglectful mother and would push away the beautiful stranger when she tried to hug him which was not frequent. Her witchery over men did not extend to her son. Nevertheless, she never left him behind and provided care for him until he died.

Colonel Blood was living with the family in Pittsburgh when Demosthenes, the orator of ancient Athens, appeared to Victoria after a hiatus of some years. He instructed her to go to New York. He foretold that in a house at 17 Great Jones Street, her destiny awaited. Of course, she went, along with extended family.

Until New York Tennie had received most of the attention and probably brought in most of the money for support of the family. Father Buck encouraged her in her indiscrete flirtations and her coarse pretensions to ladylike activities. She was pretty, cute and bold when it came to attracting men. Victoria, by all accounts, was beautiful, intense and driven to succeed at something. In New York, the way to fame was at hand, as the two women pooled their resources again. They met Cornelius Vanderbilt, the richest man in the United States.

His door was open to everyone, except doctors. He had recently lost his wife and that may have contributed to his suspicions of all doctors. But, he welcomed spiritualists, went to faith healers and consulted mediums. Of course, one look at Victoria and Tennessee probably stimulated his old pirate heart. Shortly, they were responsible for stimulating more than his heart. "Tennie's magnetic" hands took away his pains while Victoria brought him messages from the spirit world. Soon he was exchanging stock tips with Victoria who relayed them to Colonel Blood. He, in turn, acted upon them, and the financial affairs for the Claflins improved dramatically. The entire family with spouses arrived at the house on Great Jones Street to participate in the prosperity. Meanwhile, at the Vanderbilt mansion, servants began to gossip about the plump fun-loving Tennie, who could be found frequently in the morning in the Commodore's bed. He called her "my little sparrow." And, she called him her "old boy" which seemed to please him. He even proposed marriage to her, but for reasons known only to her, she refused. Some authors have suggested that his family was terrified that he would marry her. Others speculated that despite his crude social skills, he wanted to be recognized in "society" even if he did not choose to participate. So the Commodore eloped with a proper young woman, Frank (yes, Frank) Crawford in 1869. But, he did not sever his ties with the Claflin sisters.

He returned from his honeymoon when word reached him of the attempts by Jay Gould and Jim Fisk to corner the gold market in 1869. "Black Friday" did not cause financial problems for Victoria or Tennie C. because of Vanderbilt's advice. He backed them when they opened the first brokerage firm managed by women.

They were very successful. Victoria mentioned the figure of $750,000 for the first year in business. Colonel Blood probably handled all paperwork, but Victoria and Tennie met investors and seemed to manage the office with efficiency. They were called "the Bewitching Brokers" by the *New York Herald*. Of course they reveled in good publicity.

The business moved to larger quarters on 38th Street and so did the family. Even Victoria's first husband, Canning Woodhull, weak with morphine and alcohol found a haven in the new house. He took care of Byron, now sixteen, but with limited capacity from the fall on his head. New York gossips enjoyed all this news. But Victoria, who was a firm believer in "free love" principles had no problem with living with two husbands. Then there was also Stephen Pearl Andrews, who was invited to join the household while his wife was away.

Stephen Pearl Andrews was an influential intellectual who foresaw the social revolution of the twentieth century. He argued for relaxed divorce laws and promoted free love. He was an incredibly learned man who knew thirty languages, had studied medicine, the social sciences and had introduced shorthand to the United States. A mystic and a philosopher, he fit into the Claflin household, although he displaced several other Claflins. Mother Roxy hated him.

The ideas of Victoria, Andrews and Colonel Blood on spiritualism, free love and social revolution came together. But, Victoria still needed a cause which would make her famous as promised by Demosthenes. She craved fame, prominence; she wanted the world to know that she was there, in New York, demanding to be noticed. The money for her promotion was there because of the brokerage business.

In April, 1870, in a letter to the editor of the *New York Herald*, Victoria suddenly announced for the Presidency of the United States. Andrews and Blood followed up the *First Pronunciamiento* with the publication of a new paper, *The Woodhull and Claflin's Weekly*, with its motto "Upward and Onward" under the masthead. The newspaper advocated "suffrage without distinction of sex," and supported Victoria for president. She now had a cause.

Women who had been organizing to fight for the right to vote had split into two groups in 1870; neither group was too interested in Victoria's candidacy. The conservative American Woman's Suffrage Association was headed by the Reverend Henry Ward Beecher. The more liberal organization, the National Woman's Suffrage Association, asked Theodore Tilton, a protege of Beecher's, to be its president. Neither organization was aware that Tilton's wife Elizabeth had been Beecher's lover for several years. But, when a contrite Lib Tilton confessed to her husband, he could not handle her confession and confided in others when he should have shut up. The affair came back to haunt him and bring him into the web of Victoria Woodhull, who would use him and then discard him.

The ladies of the AWSA and the NWSA were obviously preoccupied with other things while Victoria continued "upward and onward." The NWSA was planning a convention to study the implications upon suffrage of the 14th and 15th amendment. Did the amendments mean "all persons born or naturalized in the United States were citizens" with the right to vote? This was the same argument used by Mary Edwards Walker who spoke at several suffrage conventions. Meanwhile, Victoria had discovered the amendments or perhaps it was Demosthenes. But, she was prepared to take action on woman's suffrage.

The suffragettes did not know that Victoria had met with representative Benjamin F. Butler of Massachusetts who was sympathetic to the movement and to Victoria. Butler loved confrontation and when he met the free thinkers on 38th Street, he, too, had another cause. An article concerning the status of women in the amendments had appeared in the *Woodhull and Claflin's Weekly* in November. Still it went unnoticed by Susan B. Anthony, off on a lecture and by Isabella Beecher Hooker who was planning the NWSA convention in January. Victoria's trip to Washington, D.C. in December to have "The Memorial of Victoria C. Woodhull" printed and presented to the U.S. Senate was also overlooked. It was sent to the Senate just before Christmas in 1870 by Senator John Spafford Harris of Louisiana and to the House of Representatives by George Washington Julian of Indiana. The petition was then referred to the Judiciary Committee of the House where the Honorable Benjamin F. Butler, a member of the committee, would make sure that Victoria was heard.

Victoria Woodhull, the first woman to speak before a congressional committee on Jan. 11, 1871, told Congressmen why existing laws should be clarified on behalf of women's suffrage.

Where were the ladies of the NWSA who were in Washington for their convention? Where were the conservatives of the AWSA? They were shocked, dismayed and incredulous when they read in the newspapers that Victoria would be speaking to the House Judiciary Committee. And, her appearance before the committee was scheduled at the same time as the opening of the NWSA convention.

The ladies ran around Washington clucking to each other. Susan B. Anthony suggested they stop this nonsensical chatter and go hear what Victoria had to say. They postponed the opening of the convention and went with Representative A. G. Riddle and Senator S. C. Pomeroy to the hearing.

In a plain black dress with a single rose at the neckline, speaking in a soft, almost inaudible voice at first, Victoria wowed the committee and the assembled ladies of the NWSA. Her speech was probably written by Stephen Pearl Andrews, but the delivery was her own. As she spoke, the clear voice, the flashing eyes, commanding voice, and convincing attitude turned the disdain into admiration. At last she had found her audience, a principle, and the beginning of fame promised by Demosthenes. She had become an orator.

When the NWSA convention opened the afternoon of Jan. 11, 1871, there on the platform sat Victoria Woodhull. The gossip about her past and the unstable family life did not go away, but it was muted by the glowing accounts of Victoria's success in advancing the suffrage cause.

During 1871 Victoria was probably influenced by Stephen Pearl Andrews to get involved in the labor movement. The group that met in the Claflin home organized themselves into Section Twelve of the International Workingmen's Association. Tennie and Victoria marched with the workers promoting women's rights and free love. Karl Marx wanted Section Twelve expelled, although the *Woodhull and Claflin's Weekly* was the first newspaper in the United States to publish his Manifesto. Was Victoria a card-carrying communist? Her newspaper remains on file in Moscow today and she was never denounced in Russia or in the United States for deviating from the party line. But she did not involve herself in labor activities after 1871. Perhaps there was insufficient publicity.

Women Short-Changed by History

At the same time, there were whispers about an awful scandal in another family that was almost an institution in late nineteenth century American life. The stories might still have remained just rumors if Henry Ward Beecher and his famous sister Harriet Beecher Stowe had not openly attacked Victoria. Henry preached occasionally against the sinful sisters, Victoria and Tennie, from his pulpit. But Harriet, using a romantic comedy poked fun at Victoria. In her novel, *My Wife and I,* Harriet presented a character Audacia Danggereyes that many people, who read the series in *The Christian Union,* thought was Victoria. So did Victoria and she was furious.

Meanwhile the should-have-been forgotten details of Henry Ward Beecher's affair with his best friend's wife, Elizabeth Tilton, were brought to light again. Theodore Tilton just could not forgive nor forget. Elizabeth Cady Stanton, a leading suffragette knew all about the affairs of Beecher. She had also been portrayed in Harriet Beecher's book as a do-gooder doomed to failure because of "an utter want of practical experience." She told Victoria of poor "Lib" Tilton. Victoria did not use the story in her paper immediately. She bided her time before striking back at the Beechers. She was proud of her accomplishments and couldn't understand why others did not appreciate her role in the suffrage movement and her stand on principle.

Her first priority was attendance at the NWSA convention in New York. Despite some protests over the prominence of The Woodhull on the platform, Victoria gave a rousing speech in which she said that if the very next Congress refused women all the legitimate results of citizenship, "We shall call another convention, frame a new constitution and erect a new government." "We mean treason; we mean secession!" "We are plotting a revolution; we will overthrow this bogus Republic . . . " "The Great Secession Speech" stirred her audience to demand reforms in every area of government. Victoria was intense, inspired and passionate. The women were so carried away with their zeal that they included in their resolutions a statement which could be regarded only as supporting "free love" between consenting adults.

Several days after Victoria's second victory in the suffrage movement, Mother Roxy, who had been living on her daughters' largess, brought Victoria's husband, Colonel Blood into court. She accused Colonel Blood of threatening her and called Victoria's household "the worst gang of free lovers." There was talk of blackmail and of the family's gypsy life. The papers jumped on every piece of juicy testimony about the Claflin family problems.

The two suffrage groups now came together to censure Susan B. Anthony and other leaders of the NWSA who sided with Victoria. She was castigated in the press. But, Victoria had her own paper and people to help her write letters to the New York papers. And, she had the inside information on the Beecher-Tilton scandal. Her threat to use that information against Beecher brought Theodore Tilton to her front door. She charmed him. He could not resist Victoria. Caught in her sexual web, he became her lover for several months. He was inspired, probably at her insistence, to write her biography in purple prose. The biography neither promoted his reputation as a writer, not did it improve Victoria's reputation for veracity. Poor Canning Woodhull could not have been the monster he was portrayed in the parnphlet, and her family probably got off better than it deserved. However, Victoria provided a haven for Woodhull when he was penniless and dying and she always took care of her dysfunctional family.

Tilton was supposed to set up a meeting with Beecher, which he did in spite of coming under Victoria's spell. Victoria later said that at the meeting with Beecher they discussed "the Social Revolution," prostitution and free love. They met again and again. In *Mrs. Satan*, Johanna Johnson quotes Victoria as saying when she and Beecher were together they did not spend their time "talking about the weather."

At this time Beecher was in his mid-fifties. A stocky man with a broad forehead, prominent nose and a full, sensual lower lip. He was also considered to be the best preacher of the day with a congregation that fought over seating in his presence. He was given to dramatic entrances with a sweep of cloak and a tossing of his hat. He thundered,

Women Short-Changed by History

he cajoled, he preached God's love. He could claim that he had more congregants on Sunday mornings than any other church in the United States.

With Victoria, he called marriage "a game of love"—she said. But how could he preach this from his pulpit?

Victoria was seeking an acknowledgement from Beecher of her "free love" principles, but he refused. No way would he introduce her at a rally proclaiming her views. Once again she turned to Tilton, who introduced her in Steinway Hall where she gave her famous Free Love speech.

She was magnificent as her voice rose over the hecklers and she dominated the hall. God is love—he gives it freely, why shouldn't we! "All that is good and commendable would continue to exist if all marriages were repealed tomorrow."

Retribution from Victorian society came swiftly. Commodore Vanderbilt withdrew advice and support. Investment bankers ignored the sisters, and the business could no longer sustain the extended family. Victoria quickly went on the lecture circuit to keep alive the *Woodhull and Claflin's Weekly*. Lampooned by the famous Thomas Nast in *Harper's Weekly*, she was now labeled Mrs. Satan when she had been called The Woodhull in previous editions. Emanie Sacks, Victoria's first biographer, called her paper "silly, venomous and sublime." It was Victoria's voice in a hostile world. It was in the paper that she was first nominated for the presidency in 1872. She had to save it.

Nothing could slow down her ambition to be famous. She turned again to her supporters in the NWSA. Victoria proposed that the suffragettes form their own political party and nominate candidates for national office who supported reform. Susan B. Anthony was suspicious of Victoria's ideas and of Victoria who had the power of her newspaper behind her. She wrote to Mrs. Stanton, president of the NWSA, that Victoria was dominated by "men spirits," and Susan B. did not want control by "men spirits." It was certainly the other way around. Victoria dominated every man who came into the same room with her.

Victoria Claflin Woodhull

Opening the *Woodhull and Claflin's Weekly* in Illinois where she was on a lecture tour, Susan B. discovered that she had signed on to the new People's Party without her consent. She was furious. There was more. The new party's first convention would be held jointly with the NWSA. Not while Susan B. was a member of the NWSA.

In May at the opening of the NWSA convention, when Victoria approached the platform, Susan B. denied the People's Party had any business there. An embarrassed Mrs. Stanton resigned as president and Susan B. was elected in her place. Victoria left the hall, but returned that evening to announce that the convention of the People's Party would meet the next morning in Apollo Hall. Victoria took over the platform in spite of Susan B.'s efforts to adjourn the proceedings. Finally, Susan B. had the janitor turn out the lights and the NWSA convention was adjourned.

The next morning belonged to Victoria. The People's Party changed its name to the Equal Rights Party and nominated Victoria C. Woodhull for President of the United States amid wild applause and almost hysterical enthusiasm.

Several candidates for vice president were suggested: Frederick Douglass, Spotted Tail and even Colonel Blood. Frederick Douglass won the nomination but the new party was dead on arrival. It had no political base other than the gathering of "free lovers," communists, suffragettes and crackpots. It is not known if Douglass was ever informed of his nomination.

The landlord at Twenty-third Street was so alarmed by his Claflin boarders that he asked them to leave. Once again, the Claflins began wandering, this time seeking shelter in New York City. There were suddenly no houses to rent. Hotels were full; boarding houses also. Victoria, her children Byron and Zulu Maud, Tennie and Colonel Blood went to the office on Broad Street and slept on the floor. When the owner of the building found them living there, he raised the rent and demanded all of it and at once. Victoria blamed the Beechers for this "persecution." She never considered her pronounced ideas on free love, social revolution, and suffrage were the reasons for the exclusion.

The situation for Victoria was so bleak that she suspended publication of the *Weekly*. In August, 1872 Victoria was sued for debt. She claimed that she had nothing left. Did her desperation force her to blackmail men and women she knew who were prominent in society? Tennie might have considered this possibility, but Victoria, a presidential candidate without a following, denied every accusation.

As president of the National Association of Spiritualism she went to the annual convention in Boston to surrender her office in a dignified manner. This did not happen. The rage over her present situation must have caused her to "lose it." The hypocrisy of the Beechers and their attacks upon her, the indignation at being refused lodging for her family, the fame that seemed within her grasp now gone, it was her turn to counter attack. She did. She told all of the Beecher-Tilton scandal. Was it obscene? By whose standards? "Obnoxious?" Possibly. Slanderous? Maybe.

Then, in a special edition of the *Weekly*, she published everything. "We would ask why should not men be held up equally to the scorn of the world . . . " New York wanted to read what Victoria had to say. The paper sold out. Johnson said in *Mrs. Satan* that some men rented their copies when no more were available.

Anthony Comstock saw a copy of the *Weekly* several days after its publication. He was a young man opposed to LUST. He came to believe that this evil lay in obscene material, which led directly to VICE. Further, the *Woodhull and Claflin's Weekly* had been sent through the mails and that was a federal offense: a law passed by Congress in 1872 made the circulation of OBSCENE material through the United States mail a misdemeanor.

Using the law, Comstock demanded the arrest of those purveyors of LUST, Victoria and Tennie. Two federal marshals, armed with a warrant halted their carriage, climbed in, and carried the sisters to a hearing in the United States Circuit Court. From there they were ordered to the Ludlow Street jail to await the findings of the grand jury.

Victoria Claflin Woodhull

Colonel Blood also was sent to the Jefferson Market prison after a warrant for libel was demanded by Luther Challis. *The Weekly* had printed a story about him and his debauchery of two underage girls.

All of these proceedings against Victoria, Tennie, and Colonel Blood were not strictly constitutional. Victoria and Tennie spent twenty-eight days without a trial. When they were released on day twenty-nine, another warrant, signed by Challis, was served. They were bailed out again, and still they were rearrested on another charge. The election of 1872 was held while Victoria was in jail. The first woman candidate for the President of the United States received 3,000 votes while in the Ludlow Street jail.

Beecher remained silent about his affair with "Lib" Tilton although letters from his brother and sisters flew back and forth. Come clean, tell the truth, they said, but the lion of Puritanism shook his mane and denied everything. Stockholders in the Puritan Church were concerned about their investment.

The lawyer William Howe was finally successful in arranging bail for Victoria and Tennie and in obtaining a writ of habeas corpus for Colonel Blood. Victoria's first thought was the *Weekly* which would "tell all" that had happened to them.

Another friend of theirs, George Francis Train, not only made money available to them, but took up the cause by printing verses from the Bible with sensational headlines. Comstock had him arrested by state authorities and into the Tombs he went. He wrote about the horrors of this infamous prison, and was elected president of a club formed by the murderers entombed there.

Other concerned voices could now be heard. Edward Clark in Troy, New York wrote that to sustain the hollow pretension of Beecher's innocence Victoria and Tennie had been thrown into jail. "The press of the nation has been confused and bullied into helping the fraud along." He continued, "Challis and Comstock—the Young Men's Christian Association and the Rake's Club—have joined hands to strangle liberty and law, honesty and truth."

Women Short-Changed by History

But, nothing silenced Victoria for long and certainly not Anthony Comstock. When Victoria planned to speak on "The Naked Truth," he deliberately brought copies of the *Weekly* deemed by him "obscene" and secured yet another indictment to prevent her speech. She disguised herself in an old gray dress and a bonnet and walked into Cooper Union. When she hobbled up to the stage, threw off her costume with a theatrical flourish and began addressing the crowd, no one moved including the police sent to arrest her. But, they did arrest her as she exited the stage. Back to prison she went. Her attorney Howe was able to make bail for her by challenging Comstock ("doing something good for Jesus every day") with "obscene" passages from Deuteronomy XXII. This chapter in the Bible deals with adultery and rape, forbidden words in the Victorian age.

Released, rearrested and released again after making $60,000 bail for an alleged misdemeanor, Victoria was physically exhausted and mentally drained. She was also broken. On a sultry June evening, returning home after delivering a letter to the editor of the *New York Star,* she felt sick. She had only tea for supper. Colonel Blood was helping her up the stairs when she collapsed. Blood oozed from her lips. Tennie thought she was dead. Victoria was in a coma for four days.

"At the door of death," stated the *Democrat.* "The wicked Woodhull is dying."

But she did not die.

Instead, several weeks later, pale and nervous, Victoria entered the court room on June 26, 1873, the day of the obscenity trial. She emerged victorious. The judge ruled that no evidence had been presented against her on the obscenity charge. The jury found the defendants, "Not guilty." There were no victory statements. Instead Victoria commented that perhaps she had "touched bottom at last."

Not yet. The alcoholism that had caused the death of her first husband became manifest in sister Utica. Violent rages and intemperate actions fueled by alcohol and jealousy were symptoms of Utica's problems in the chaotic Claflin clan. She died suddenly after the trial.

Victoria and Tennie C. immediately arranged for an autopsy. Utica died of Bright's disease, not a sexually transmitted one.

Victoria mourned her sister.

Although she continued her passionate, even outrageous comments in speeches, something new now was added in the texts: a search for permanency or possibly immortality. "The Scarecrows of Sexual Freedom" called by one reporter "the most outrageous address ever yet delivered by her." She said, "in a perfected sexuality shall continuous life be found." In another speech before the spiritualists, a man in the audience accused her of prostitution to gain her own ends. She answered him by asking where he had been in her hour of need, then continued that perfect sex was "the Elixir of Life," and the continuity of life.

While Victoria was lecturing on the social revolution, sex education in schools and free love, the Challis suit for libel was scheduled for trial. Charles Brooke, her young, Irish lawyer had the trial postponed until March 5, 1874. The judge may have been biased against Victoria. Certainly he used the bench as a platform for lectures on morality. But, Victoria had her young daughter, Zulu Maud, seated beside her. She could cry and look pathetic as her mother was sent to the Tombs every night because the judge refused to set bail.

The judge instructed the jury that its verdict should be guilty. It deliberated all night and after one hundred ballots found Victoria, Tennie and Colonel Blood not guilty of libel. Naturally, the judge was outraged and said he was ashamed of the jury. Victoria hugged everyone, except the judge, and returned to the lecture circuit to pay her lawyer fees and keep the *Weekly* alive.

While she was condemning marriage in her speeches on the West Coast, the Plymouth Church elders tried to end the Beecher-Tilton scandal once and for all. They appointed a committee of investigation, approved by Beecher, to determine if "Lib" Tilton had indeed been seduced by their pastor. Would Victoria be called before the committee? The committee was courteous, but no thank you. When asked about

Women Short-Changed by History

her previous statements about Beecher, Victoria said, "No comment." And, without any money of her own, she took Colonel Blood, Mother Roxy, Zulu Maud on a tour of France. Also included was a young lover, Bennie Tucker, later publisher of *Liberty* magazine, who wrote in his memoirs about the trip and Tennie's advances to him. Where did Victoria find the money to pay for this extended vacation?

Immediately upon hearing the committee's report, Theodore Tilton swore out a complaint against Beecher charging him with alienating his wife's affections and asking $100,000 in compensation for the loss.

Victoria, after her holiday in Europe, immediately went on another lecture tour, leaving people to speculate as to where she had found the money for the family's vacation.

She returned to New York in time for what was then called the "most famous trial in American history" in January, 1875. Theodore Tilton sued Henry Ward Beecher for alienating the affections of his wife, Elizabeth. The trial ran one hundred and twelve days, ending with a hung jury. The newspapers had a wonderful time. Of course, The Woodhull's name was prominent. She was subpoenaed by the defendant because of certain letters from Tilton in her possession. At her only appearance in that courtroom, she produced several letters from Tilton to herself. Both sides had reason to fear the letters. But, Victoria claimed that most of them had been taken when Comstock and the government ransacked her office. She was not asked to testify. Florid, flamboyant Beecher did. Questioned 897 times, he could not remember, could not recollect or did not know. The jury couldn't decide either. The case was not retried. The reputations of both men suffered, but Tilton was ruined. He fled to France and remained there until his death. "Lib" Tilton was forgotten by both men.

Victoria had the last word on the affair: "I believe that Mr. Tilton would make quite a man if he should live to grow up."

She followed up this comment with a letter to the editor of the New York *Herald* which hinted at some manner of conversion on her part. It seemed that Jesus came to her in the Ludlow Street jail, cautioning her to "WAIT!" For what? For the new Victoria to emerge, one who leaned more upon mother Roxy and less upon Colonel Blood. Her lecture tours now encouraged purity and a defense of marriage, but her audiences had been stimulated by SIN and were now apathetic about purity. Editors of the *Weekly* deserted her. They were not interested in her writings about purity. Even the spiritualists, Victoria's most ardent followers, left her after she wrote an expose of manifestations for the paper. The ultimate treason appeared in the June 10, 1876 edition of the *Weekly*. Victoria Woodhull maintained that she had not really been a supporter of "free love," but had been an advocate of "the institution of marriage as a divine provision." When she printed this view on the sanctity of marriage in the *Weekly,* no one bought the paper.

After six years of publication, she ended the *Weekly*. Several months later, she divorced Colonel Blood, accusing him of adultery. He did not deny, affirm, nor fight the charges. He never spoke against Victoria nor challenged her in any way as long as he lived.

Victoria was metamorphosed into a new creature.

Once again she faced lecture halls to support her family. She was desperate for money. Exhausted, worn, probably ailing physically, she still advanced to the podium like a queen. Dressed in black, with the Bible in hand and a white rose at the neck of her silk dress, she urged people in Dallas, Texas to be "pure." "Free love is the free love of God to the world." Enough of social revolution.

The depression following the panic of 1873 brought Victoria to begging former subscribers of the *Weekly* for assistance. Nothing was forthcoming.

Then, in January of 1877, the ailing mogul Cornelius Vanderbilt died leaving a fortune estimated at $105,000,000—quite sizable for the nineteenth century. Most of it, $90 million, went to son William, but another son and two daughters were determined to challenge the will. They wanted more than a meager million each. Was their father of sound mind in his later years? They recalled his indulgence of Victoria Woodhull and Tennie C. and his reliance upon Spiritualism. He even left these two sisters in charge of money to further the cause. Victoria and Tennie discovered he owed them money too, long past due, with interest added, for funds they had given to him to invest and for "speculative purposes"—maybe totaling half a million. Victoria and Tennie were prepared to sue unless their claim against the Commodore's estate was paid.

Who knows what transactions were made with William Vanderbilt to prevent the sisters' court appearance as a challenge to the will. Although penniless early in 1877, in late 1877, the family, Victoria, Tennie, and the two children, Zulu Maud and Byron, left for England with no plans for returning to the United States. Buck and Roxy stayed briefly in New York. Buck was needed in court to testify about the Commodore's relationship with Tennie. Quickly, the judge decided to exclude most of what he thought Buck might say. And, the next day, the well-heeled Dr. R. Buckman Claflin and wife joined his daughters in London.

They rented a nice house in a fashionable suburb of London. Here, Victoria regained her health and planned for her entry into the English lecture circuit. With a new speech, "The Human Body: The Temple of God," she began her tour in St. James Hall in London.

Rested and feeling good, Victoria was, as always, the gifted orator. At one London lecture, a young, handsome conservative banker, John Biddulph Martin, Esq., heard Victoria and was "charmed with her high intellect and fascinated by her manner." He left the lecture hall that evening determined to marry Victoria Woodhull.

And, so, the second part of her life began as she attempted to reinvent herself and become acceptable to the young Mr. Martin and to English society. She wrote to London papers, disavowing "free love." She presented herself as a presidential candidate in 1880, probably to impress Martin's mother. But, she never left England to campaign and received no votes in the United States. It is doubtful if Martin's mother was impressed. She refused to give her consent to the engagement while she lived, which was six more years.

It was Colonel Blood's turn to take the blame for Victoria's life in the United States as it had been that of poor Canning Woodhull twenty years earlier. Victoria even claimed she was a victim of "slow poisoning." Colonel Blood was devastated, but like Canning Woodhull, he never said a word against Victoria.

She began a new magazine, the *Woodhull and Claflin's Journal,* in which she proclaimed her innocence of "slanderous libels" and "vile traducers." One issue in January 1881 was all she published. She attacked Stephen Pearl Andrews as an "Arch Blasphemer." In the same year she returned to the United States in an attempt to silence sarcastic letters and comments by people who had known her in "the old days." Several sources told of her passing Colonel Blood on the street and moving past him quickly with eyes averted. (Four years after the chance encounter with Victoria, Colonel Blood married a respectable widow and left several months later on an expedition to Africa, searching for a gold mine. There he died of a fever after Christmas in 1885. His son-in-law brought back the Colonel's body for burial in Brooklyn. He had never made a derogatory remark about Victoria in his life. His friends surmised that in his search for gold, he was really looking for a way to bring her back to him.)

Victoria's efforts during the next two years were toward respectability and social acceptance. Her task was made more difficult because of a novel by fellow American, Henry James. In the thinly disguised satire, *The Siege of London,* James describes the efforts of Nancy Headway, an American adventuress, determined to marry into a prominent English family. Despite her shady past, Nancy was utterly charming, clever, and capable of working "a certain spell." Victoria Woodhull and Nancy Headway were both successful in explaining away their pasts. Shortly after the death of the mother of John Biddulph Martin, he and Victoria were married on October 31, 1883.

Tennie C. Claflin, now calling herself Tennessee, often joined her sister at the Martin's elegant home at 17 Hyde Park Gate. There they concocted a family pedigree relating themselves to George Washington and to King Robert III of Scotland, King James of England and Alexander Hamilton. English society was not amused. But, Mr. Martin obviously was. Victoria was said to have one of London's best cooks, and that was merely another to keep him enthralled, which he was.

After Victoria's quiet marriage to the respectable banker, Tennessee met an elderly, rich, titled Englishman, Francis Cook, who had an interest in spiritualism. From Mr. Cook's dead wife came a message, through Tennessee, that he should get married—to Tennessee. And, he did. She went to live at his mansion on the Thames River, although they spent time at his marble castle in Portugal where King Luis had conferred upon him the title Viscount of Montserrat. The castle with its extensive gardens was a showplace. But, more important to him was Doughty House in England with one of the finest art collections in the world. When Mr. Cook endowed an artists' house in Kensington, a grand party was given which the Prince and Princess of Wales attended, making it a huge success. Francis Cook was made a baronet by Queen Victoria for the founding of Kensington House for women students of music and art. Tennessee could call herself Lady Cook.

It was time for everything to end well for Victoria and Tennessee, but this was not to be with the Claflin family. Another sister became embroiled in overturning her own daughter's will, long after she had abandoned the child. The "ladies" of English society refused to associate with the two sisters, and one of the ladies even paid investigators to dig up their past, which was not difficult to do. The newspapers had always printed the scandals about "Mrs. Satan" and there was the *Woodhull and Claflin's Weekly* containing her opinions on everything, including free love. The Woodhull sisters were accused, falsely, of extortion when London newspapers confused their names with criminals. The press buried an apology in the back pages of the papers.

Victoria expended her time and energy, obsessed with articles, magazines and pamphlets of self-justification. She lost the presidential election of 1888 to Benjamin Harrison. She did not receive any votes. But, neither did she campaign in the United States.

Two years later, she began a series of voyages across the Atlantic to "set the record straight," but these trips usually ended in disaster. The first trip was especially upsetting. She challenged Police Inspector Thomas Byrnes over a nasty article in the *Brooklyn Eagle*. He admitted he wrote the article, refused to retract it or say that someone else had written it. He told poor Mr. Martin to sue him, but, of course, Victoria could not allow that because the publicity would bring to light her past history! The trip was cut short, but not before Tennessee was branded as a fugitive from justice. She had been charged with manslaughter and fraud more than twenty-five years previously. Authorities in Ottawa, Illinois, were excited about charging Lady Cook with contributing to the death of a cancer patient by claiming to heal her spiritually and with Papa Buck's mustard plaster. But, what sent the Martins scurrying back to England with their one hundred pieces of luggage were biographies of the sisters that contained every trashy story collected from acquaintances and culled from newspaper articles about their activities. The stories were probably paid for by their social enemies in London.

Tennessee's reaction to all this was to ignore it and to donate her time and money to charities, and to exhibit to the world the famous Doughty House art collection.

Victoria responded to the latest and worst insults, which her husband couldn't have ignored, with a physical collapse. Once before she had been close to death when she had perceived her world crumbling around her. Of course, she recovered. At the age of fifty-four, she began another newspaper, *The Humanitarian,* and she ran for the presidency for the fifth and last time in 1892. Although she tried to become the candidate of the NWSA again, they knew Victoria and refused her attempts to lead them. She organized Victoria Leagues who supported her "humanitarian platform." But, once again, she received no votes.

It is almost painful to watch Victoria and her husband demand respectability through a series of lawsuits that, at times, seemed ridiculous. Obviously not to her. The single-minded strength she put into these efforts drained her physically and emotionally, and yet she came no nearer her goal of erasing a past that had been laid out for the world to see. She had no women friends in whom she might have confided. Tennie was having a wonderful time as Lady Cook. Zulu Maud she tied to her with bonds of sacrifice. Did Victoria have the ability to love?

One more attempt was made to silence the past that would not go away because she would drag it up, again and again. This time the venerable British Museum, which today contains many of the pamphlets and newspaper articles about Mrs. Martin, was brought into court, charged with libel. Especially onerous to her was the biography of Henry Ward Beecher, which called Victoria a blackmailer. The book was on the library shelves. One of the museum's lawyers commented that the action brought by Victoria was merely "to allow this lady to make a statement in the box to contradict a number of publications offensive to her." This was exactly what she did.

The museum, being unaware of the books or that books contained libelous statements, was fined twenty shillings by the British Court and Mrs. Martin considered herself "thoroughly vindicated during the trial."

Family problems involving Zulu Maud and her cousin and aunt forced Mr. and Mrs. Martin to once again go to New York. But by this time, Mr. Martin must have hated these dramatic visitations to the United States. This would be the last time for him. When he returned to London, he published his book about the family bank, *The Grasshopper of Lombard Street.* It was well-received as were his other monographs on finance. Mr. Martin was known and highly regarded in financial circles, while Victoria was ignored. She brooded over the dullness of her existence. If she sought the stuffiness of English society, that's what she got, and she didn't like it. Her pamphlets and newspaper, *The Humanitarian,* lacked the old fire and were dull, too. But, she kept publishing them. It is ironic that she became what she most disliked.

Several years later Victoria's husband, the shy, bewitched, reserved banker John Biddulph Martin died. Diagnosed with pneumonia, he went to the Canary Islands to recuperate in the sunshine. It was one of the few times that Victoria did not accompany him. He died in Las Palmas in March, 1897. He requested cremation. Victoria became a very wealthy widow.

Tennessee's husband died in 1901, leaving her enough money to enjoy the life to which she had become accustomed. Somehow, the two sisters, after their lives of shared disappointments, tragedies and victories, disassociated themselves from each other. Tennie traveled and enjoyed the company of young relatives. She was still pretty and, in pastel gowns and lacy bonnets, looked almost fragile. However, the old Tennie, robust and fun-loving, was never far away. She chose to live in Portugal, but frequently traveled to the United States. The palace, near Cintra, Portugal, was host to Sir Thomas Beecham. In the gardens, he courted Utica Celestia, grandniece of Tennessee and Victoria. Their marriage was not a happy one, ending in divorce. Tennessee later lived with Utica Celestia in London and died there in 1923. Every line of her obituary in the *London Times* and the *New York Times* was favorable to Lady Cook, Viscountess of Monserrat.

After Mr. Martin's death, Victoria packed up her belongings, Byron and Zula Maud, and moved from London to the English countryside.

From the Biddulph's Manor House, Victoria reigned supreme over Bredon's Norton and its 1,500 acres. She was in her element. With time, money and her domineering will she proceeded to tell farmers how to improve their yield and gardeners how to grow better roses. The annual flower show, today an agricultural fair for the region, was a product of her determination. She let part of the estate to women only and taught them to farm. She had a village school built on the estate and hired trained kindergarten teachers when the education committee of the district was committed to "the old way," and did not listen to Victoria's ideas on education.

Victoria bought one of the first motor cars in England and went speeding through the countryside. She kept three cars in the stables.

She was interested in aviation and was a member of the Women's Aerial League of Great Britain. She authored more pamphlets preaching purity and virtue. She filled the Manor House with antiques. She entertained. She was generous and charming. She could afford to be, but then, she had always been enthusiastic about her projects.

When World War I was declared in Europe in 1914, Victoria, the organizer, arranged benefits for the Red Cross. She recruited lecturers, had teas for wounded soldiers, and settled Belgian refugees. She was accepted and admired "because she managed her estate so well." She had repaired the houses of Bredon's Norton, provided sanitation, and made road repairs. All she required in exchange was good publicity.

Most of this was gained when she became involved in the Sulgrave Committee of the Anglo-American Society. The committee purchased the home of George Washington's ancestors in England. Victoria contributed generously to the restoration of the manor. She also promised the committee to give the Old Manor House on her estate, the lodge and the Old Tithe Barn to the organization. She dangled this promise before the committee. On her ninetieth birthday, she said that it would receive title to these buildings. They are now listed as National Trust properties.

"A splinter of the indestructible" a reporter had described her during her first run for the White House. On her eighty-fifth birthday, she was interviewed again. There was no one left to say that she was not "The United States Mother of Woman's Suffrage." No one remembered her activities in the labor movement, communist marches in New York, speeches on free love, publisher of Karl Marx's *Manifesto,* membership in Section Twelve of the International Working Men's Association and Social Revolution. She was indeed a respected member of British society.

Victoria Claflin Woodhull Blood Martin was found dead the morning of June 10, 1927, just before her ninetieth birthday. According to her wishes, her body was cremated and her ashes scattered in the ocean. Her son, Byron, had died in his seventies. Zulu Maud, who had promised her mother that she would never marry, was the sole heir to the Martin fortune, including Bredon's Norton.

The *Times* of London carried no hint of scandal in Victoria's obituary. Instead, it mentioned an exceptional education that included the study of law, medicine and surgery in addition to banking interests and scientific agriculture. Anyone who had known Victoria "in the old days" would have found the obituary incredible. Her old lover and late enemy, Bennie Tucker, still alive, commented, "She would have been glorious, in she hadn't been infamous."

The last word on Victoria belonged to the Rector of Bredon as he delivered the memorial address:

"We have been privileged to have one of the world's greatest personalities among us."

Victoria would have liked that as her epitaph.

Selected Bibliography

Sachs, Ermanie. *The Terrible Siren.* New York: Harper and Brothers Publishers, 1928. The first in-depth book written about Victoria Woodhull. Sachs interviewed people who remembered Victoria and her family.

Abbott, Lyman. *Henry Ward Beecher.* New York: Houghton Mifflin Company, 1903.

Andrews, Wayne. *The Vanderbilt Legend.* New York: Harcourt Brace, 1941.

Brown, Heywood and Mary Leech. *Anthony Comstock.* New York: Albert and Charles Boni, 1927.

Clews, Henry. *Fifty Years in Wall Street.* New York: Irving Publishing Company, 1908.

Darewine, G. S. *Synopsis of the Lives of Victoria Woodhull and Tennessee Claflin.* London: J. H. Corthesy, 1891.

James, Henry. *The Great Short Novels of Henry James.* Philip Rahv, editor. New York: Dial Press, 1944.

Johnson, Johanna. *Mrs. Satan.* New York: G. P. Putnam's Sons, 1967.

Marberry, M. M. *Vicky.* New York: Funk and Wagnalls, 1967.

"Death of Victoria Woodhull." *The Nation,* 19 June 1927.

Shaplen, Robert. "That Was New York: Beecher-Tilton Case." *New Yorker,* 12 June 1954.

Cheshire, H. and M. "Woman for President?" *New York Times Magazine,* 27 May 1956.

Shaplen, Robert. *Free Love and Heavenly Sinners.* New York: Alfred A. Knopf, 1954.

Tilton, Theodore. *Life of Victoria Claflin Woodhull.* New York: Golden Age, 1891.

Woodhull, Victoria C. *The Argument for Women's Electoral Rights Under Amendments XIV and XV: A Review of My Work at*

Washington D. C. in 1870–1871. London: G. Norman and Son, 1887.

Woodhull, Victoria C. *Origins, Tendencies and Principles of Government.* New York: Woodhull, Claflin and Company, 1871. Contains lecture on Constitutional Equality and also the secession speech at Apollo Hall.

Miscellaneous printed materials available at the New York Public Library, including copies of the newspaper *Woodhull and Claflins's Weekly.* Much of the *Weekly* was probably written by Stephen Pearl Andrews.

for Melody,

the child and the artist